Introduction to Apache Flink

*Stream Processing for
Real Time and Beyond*

Ellen Friedman and Kostas Tzoumas

Beijing · Boston · Farnham · Sebastopol · Tokyo

Introduction to Apache Flink

by Ellen Friedman and Kostas Tzoumas

Published by O'Reilly Media, Inc., 1005 Gravenstein Highway North, Sebastopol, CA 95472.

O'Reilly books may be purchased for educational, business, or sales promotional use. Online editions are also available for most titles (*http://safaribooksonline.com*). For more information, contact our corporate/institutional sales department: 800-998-9938 or *corporate@oreilly.com*.

Editor: Shannon Cutt	**Interior Designer:** David Futato
Production Editor: Holly Bauer Forsyth	**Cover Designer:** Karen Montgomery
Copyeditor: Holly Bauer Forsyth	**Illustrator:** Rebecca Panzer
Proofreader: Octal Publishing, Inc.	

September 2016:   First Edition

Revision History for the First Edition

2016-09-01:   First Release
2016-10-20:   Second Release

978-1-491-97658-6

[LSI]

Table of Contents

Preface

There's a flood of interest in learning how to analyze streaming data in large-scale systems, partly because there are situations in which the time-value of data makes real-time analytics so attractive. But gathering in-the-moment insights made possible by very low-latency applications is just one of the benefits of high-performance stream processing.

In this book, we offer an introduction to Apache Flink, a highly innovative open source stream processor with a surprising range of capabilities that help you take advantage of stream-based approaches. Flink not only enables fault-tolerant, truly real-time analytics, it can also analyze historical data and greatly simplify your data pipeline. Perhaps most surprising is that Flink lets you do streaming analytics as well as batch jobs, both with one technology. Flink's expressivity and robust performance make it easy to develop applications, and Flink's architecture makes those easy to maintain in production.

Not only do we explain what Flink can do, we also describe how people are using it, including in production. Flink has an active and rapidly growing open international community of developers and users. The first Flink-only conference, called Flink Forward, was held in Berlin in October 2015, the second is scheduled for September 2016, and there are Apache Flink meetups around the world, with new use cases being widely reported.

How to Use This Book

This book will be useful for both nontechnical and technical readers. No specialized skills or previous experience with stream processing are necessary to understand the explanations of underlying concepts of Flink's designs and capabilities, although a general familiarity with big data systems is helpful. To be able to use sample code or the tutorials referenced in the book, experience with Java or Scala is needed, but the key concepts underlying these examples are explained clearly in this book even without needing to understand the code itself.

Chapters 1–3 provide a basic explanation of the needs that motivated Flink's development and how it meets them, the advantages of a stream-first architecture, and an overview of Flink design. Chapter 4–Appendix A provide a deeper, technical explanation of Flink's capabilities.

Conventions Used in This Book

This icon indicates a general note.

This icon signifies a tip or suggestion.

This icon indicates a warning or caution.

CHAPTER 1

Why Apache Flink?

*Our best understanding comes when our conclusions fit evidence, and
that is most effectively done when our analyses fit the way life happens.*

Many of the systems we need to understand—cars in motion emitting GPS signals, financial transactions, interchange of signals
between cell phone towers and people busy with their smartphones,
web traffic, machine logs, measurements from industrial sensors
and wearable devices—all proceed as a continuous flow of events. If
you have the ability to efficiently analyze streaming data at large
scale, you're in a much better position to understand these systems
and to do so in a timely manner. In short, streaming data is a better
fit for the way we live.

It's natural, therefore, to want to collect data as a stream of events
and to process data as a stream, but up until now, that has not been
the standard approach. Streaming isn't entirely new, but it has been
considered as a specialized and often challenging approach. Instead,
enterprise data infrastructure has usually assumed that data is
organized as finite sets with beginnings and ends that at some point
become complete. It's been done this way largely because this
assumption makes it easier to build systems that store and process
data, but it is in many ways a forced fit to the way life happens.

So there is an appeal to processing data as streams, but that's been
difficult to do well, and the challenges of doing so are even greater
now as people have begun to work with data at very large scale
across a wide variety of sectors. It's a matter of physics that with

large-scale distributed systems, exact consistency and certain knowledge of the order of events are necessarily limited. But as our methods and technologies evolve, we can strive to make these limitations innocuous in so far as they affect our business and operational goals.

That's where Apache Flink comes in. Built as open source software by an open community, Flink provides stream processing for large-volume data, and it also lets you handle batch analytics, with one technology.

It's been engineered to overcome certain tradeoffs that have limited the effectiveness or ease-of-use of other approaches to processing streaming data.

In this book, we'll investigate potential advantages of working well with data streams so that you can see if a stream-based approach is a good fit for your particular business goals. Some of the sources of streaming data and some of the situations that make this approach useful may surprise you. In addition, the will book help you understand Flink's technology and how it tackles the challenges of stream processing.

In this chapter, we explore what people want to achieve by analyzing streaming data and some of the challenges of doing so at large scale. We also introduce you to Flink and take a first look at how people are using it, including in production.

Consequences of Not Doing Streaming Well

Who needs to work with streaming data? Some of the first examples that come to mind are people working with sensor measurements or financial transactions, and those are certainly situations where stream processing is useful. But there are much more widespread sources of streaming data: clickstream data that reflects user behavior on websites and machine logs for your own data center are two familiar examples. In fact, streaming data sources are essentially ubiquitous—it's just that there has generally been a disconnect between data from continuous events and the consumption of that data in batch-style computation. That's now changing with the development of new technologies to handle large-scale streaming data.

Still, if it has historically been a challenge to work with streaming data at very large scale, why now go to the trouble to do it, and to do it well? Before we look at what has changed—the new architecture and emerging technologies that support working with streaming data—let's first look at the consequences of *not* doing streaming well.

Retail and Marketing

In the modern retail world, sales are often represented by clicks from a website, and this data may arrive at large scale, continuously but not evenly. Handling it well at scale using older techniques can be difficult. Even building batch systems to handle these dataflows is challenging—the result can be an enormous and complicated workflow. The result can be dropped data, delays, or misaggregated results. How might that play out in business terms?

Imagine that you're reporting sales figures for the past quarter to your CEO. You don't want to have to recant later because you over-reported results based on inaccurate figures. If you don't deal with clickstream data well, you may end up with inaccurate counts of website traffic—and that in turn means inaccurate billing for ad placement and performance figures.

Airline passenger services face the similar challenge of handling huge amounts of data from many sources that must be quickly and accurately coordinated. For example, as passengers check in, data must be checked against reservation information, luggage handling and flight status, as well as billing. At this scale, it's not easy to keep up unless you have robust technology to handle streaming data. The recent major service outages with three of the top four airlines can be directly attributed to problems handling real-time data at scale.

Of course many related problems—such as the importance of not double-booking hotel rooms or concert tickets—have traditionally been handled effectively with databases, but often at considerable expense and effort. The costs can begin to skyrocket as the scale of data grows, and database response times are too slow for some situations. Development speed may suffer from lack of flexibility and come to a crawl in large and complex or evolving systems. Basically, it is difficult to react in a way that lets you keep up with life as it happens while maintaining consistency and affordability in large-scale systems.

Fortunately, modern stream processors can often help address these issues in new ways, working well at scale, in a timely manner, and less expensively. Stream processing also invites exploration into doing new things, such as building real-time recommendation systems to react to what people are buying *right now*, as part of deciding *what else* they are likely to want. It's not that stream processors replace databases—far from it; rather, they can in certain situations address roles for which databases are not a great fit. This also frees up databases to be used for locally specific views of current state of business. This shift is explained more thoroughly in our discussion of stream-first architecture in Chapter 2.

The Internet of Things

The Internet of Things (IoT) is an area where streaming data is common and where low-latency data delivery and processing, along with accuracy of data analysis, is often critical. Sensors in various types of equipment take frequent measurements and stream those to data centers where real-time or near real–time processing applications will update dashboards, run machine learning models, issue alerts, and provide feedback for many different services.

The transportation industry is another example where it's important to do streaming well. State-of-the-art train systems, for instance, rely on sensor data communicated from tracks to trains and from trains to sensors along the route; together, reports are also communicated back to control centers. Measurements include train speed and location, plus information from the surroundings for track conditions. If this streaming data is not processed correctly, adjustments and alerts do not happen in time to adjust to dangerous conditions and avoid accidents.

Another example from the transportation industry are "smart" or connected cars, which are being designed to communicate data via cell phone networks, back to manufacturers. In some countries (i.e., Nordic countries, France, the UK, and beginning in the US), connected cars even provide information to insurance companies and, in the case of race cars, send information back to the pit via a radio frequency (RF) link for analysis. Some smartphone applications also provide real-time traffic updates shared by millions of drivers, as suggested in Figure 1-1.

Figure 1-1. The time-value of data comes into consideration in many situations including IoT data used in transportation. Real-time traffic information shared by millions of drivers relies on reasonably accurate analysis of streaming data that is processed in a timely manner. (Image credit © 2016 Friedman)

The IoT is also having an impact in utilities. Utility companies are beginning to implement smart meters that send updates on usage periodically (e.g., every 15 minutes), replacing the old meters that are read manually once a month. In some cases, utility companies are experimenting with making measurements every 30 seconds. This change to smart meters results in a huge amount of streaming data, and the potential benefits are large. The advantages include the ability to use machine learning models to detect usage anomalies caused by equipment problems or energy theft. Without efficient ways to deliver and accurately process streaming data at high throughput and with very low latencies, these new goals cannot be met.

Other IoT projects also suffer if streaming is not done well. Large equipment such as turbines in a wind farm, manufacturing equipment, or pumps in a drilling operation—these all rely on analysis of sensor measurements to provide malfunction alerts. The consequences of not handling stream analysis well and with adequate latency in these cases can be costly or even catastrophic.

Telecom

The telecommunications industry is a special case of IoT data, with its widespread use of streaming event data for a variety of purposes across geo-distributed regions. If a telecommunications company cannot process streaming data well, it will fail to preemptively reroute usage surges to alternative cell towers or respond quickly to outages. Anomaly detection to processes streaming data is important to this industry—in this case, to detect dropped calls or equipment malfunctions.

Banking and Financial Sector

The potential problems caused by not doing stream processing well are particularly evident in banking and financial settings. A retail bank would not want customer transactions to be delayed or to be miscounted and therefore result in erroneous account balances. The old-fashioned term "bankers' hours" referred to the need to close up a bank early in the afternoon in order to freeze activity so that an accurate tally could be made before the next day's business. That batch style of business is long gone. Transactions and reporting today must happen quickly and accurately; some new banks even offer immediate, real-time push notifications and mobile banking access anytime, anywhere. In a global economy, it's increasingly important to be able to meet the needs of a 24-hour business cycle.

What happens if a financial institution does not have applications that can recognize anomalous behavior in user activity data with sensitive detection in real time? Fraud detection for credit card transactions requires timely monitoring and response. Being able to detect unusual login patterns that signal an online phishing attack can translate to huge savings by detecting problems in time to mitigate loss.

The time-value of data in many situations makes low-latency or real-time stream processing highly desirable, as long as it's also accurate and efficient.

Goals for Processing Continuous Event Data

Being able to process data with very low latency is not the only advantage of effective stream processing. A wishlist for stream processing not only includes high throughput with low latency, but the processing system also needs to be able to deal with interruptions. A great streaming technology should be able to restart after a failure in a manner that produces accurate results; in other words, there's an advantage to being fault-tolerant with exactly-once guarantees.

Furthermore, the method used to achieve this level of fault tolerance preferably should not carry a lot of overhead cost in the absence of failures. It's useful to be able to recognize sessions based on when the events occur rather than an arbitrary processing interval and to be able to track events in the correct order. It's also important for such a system to be easy for developers to use, both in writing code and in fixing bugs, and it should be easily maintained. Also important is that these systems produce correct results with respect to the time that events happen in the real world—for example, being able to handle streams of events that arrive out of order (an unfortunate reality), and being able to deterministically replace streams (e.g., for auditing or debugging purposes).

Evolution of Stream Processing Technologies

The disconnect between continuous data production and data consumption in finite batches, while making the job of systems builders easier, has shifted the complexity of managing this disconnect to the users of the systems: the application developers and DevOps teams that need to use and manage this infrastructure.

To manage this disconnect, some users have developed their own stream processing systems. In the open source space, a pioneer in stream processing is the Apache Storm project that started with Nathan Marz and a team at startup BackType (later acquired by Twitter) before being accepted into the Apache Software Foundation. Storm brought the possibility for stream processing with very low latency, but this real-time processing involved tradeoffs: high throughput was hard to achieve, and Storm did not provide the level of correctness that is often needed. In other words, it did not have exactly-once guarantees for maintaining accurate state, and even the guarantees that Storm could provide came at a high overhead.

Overview of Lambda Architecture: Advantages and Limitations

The need for affordable scale drove people to distributed file systems such as HDFS and batch-based computing (MapReduce jobs). But that approach made it difficult to deal with low-latency insights. Development of real-time stream processing technology with Apache Storm helped address the latency issue, but not as a complete solution. For one thing, Storm did not guarantee state consistency with exactly-once processing and did not handle event-time processing. People who had these needs were forced to implement these features in their application code.

A hybrid view of data analytics that mixed these approaches offered one way to deal with these challenges. This hybrid, called *Lambda architecture*, provided delayed but accurate results via batch Map-Reduce jobs and an in-the-moment preliminary view of new results via Storm's processing.

The Lambda architecture is a helpful framework for building big data applications, but it is not sufficient. For example, with a Lambda system based on MapReduce and HDFS, there is a time window, in hours, when inaccuracies due to failures are visible. Lambda architectures need the same business logic to be coded twice, in two different programming APIs: once for the batch system and once for the streaming system. This leads to two codebases that represent the same business problem, but have different kinds of bugs. In practice, this is very difficult to maintain.

To compute values that depend on multiple streaming events, it is necessary to retain data from one event to another. This retained data is known as the state of the computation. Accurate handling of state is essential for consistency in computation. The ability to accurately update state after a failure or interruption is a key to fault tolerance.

It's hard to maintain fault-tolerant stream processing that has high throughput with very low latency, but the need for guarantees of accurate state motivated a clever compromise: what if the stream of data from continuous events were broken into a series of small, atomic batch jobs? If the batches were cut small enough—so-called "micro-batches"—your computation could approximate true streaming. The latency could not quite reach real time, but latencies of several seconds or even subseconds for very simple applications would be possible. This is the approach taken by Apache Spark Streaming, which runs on the Spark batch engine.

More important, with micro-batching, you can achieve exactly-once guarantees of state consistency. If a micro-batch job fails, it can be rerun. This is much easier than would be true for a continuous stream-processing approach. An extension of Storm, called Storm Trident, applies micro-batch computation on the underlying stream processor to provide exactly-once guarantees, but at a substantial cost to latency.

However, simulating streaming with periodic batch jobs leads to very fragile pipelines that mix DevOps with application development concerns. The time that a periodic batch job takes to finish is tightly coupled with the timing of data arrival, and any delays can cause inconsistent (a.k.a. wrong) results. The underlying problem with this approach is that time is only managed implicitly by the part of the system that creates the small jobs. Frameworks like Spark Streaming mitigate some of the fragility, but not entirely, and the sensitivity to timing relative to batches still leads to poor latency and a user experience where one needs to think a lot about performance in the application code.

These tradeoffs between desired capabilities have motivated continued attempts to improve existing processors (for example, the development of Storm Trident to try to overcome some of the limitations of Storm). When existing processors fall short, the burden is placed on the application developer to deal with any issues that result. An example is the case of micro-batching, which does not provide an excellent fit between the natural occurrence of sessions in event data and the processor's need to window data only as multiples of the batch time (recovery interval). With less flexibility and expressivity, development time is slower and operations take more effort to maintain properly.

This brings us to Apache Flink, a data processor that removes many of these tradeoffs and combines many of the desired traits needed to efficiently process data from continuous events. The combination of some of Flink's capabilities is illustrated in Figure 1-2.

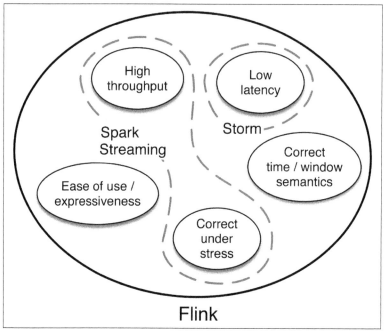

Figure 1-2. One of the strengths of Apache Flink is the way it combines many desirable capabilities that have previously required a tradeoff in other projects. Apache Storm, in contrast, provides low latency, but at present does not provide high throughput and does not support correct handling of state when failures happen. The micro-batching approach of Apache Spark Streaming achieves fault tolerance with high throughput, but at the cost of very low latency/real-time processing, inability to fit windows to naturally occurring sessions, and some challenges with expressiveness.

As is the case with Storm and Spark Streaming, other new technologies in the field of stream processing offer some useful capabilities, but it's hard to find one with the combination of traits that Flink offers. Apache Samza, for instance, is another early open source processor for streaming data, but it has also been limited to at-least-once guarantees and a low-level API. Similarly, Apache Apex provides some of the benefits of Flink, but not all (e.g., it is limited to a low-level programming API, it does not support event time, and it does not have support for batch computations). And none of these projects have been able to attract an open source community comparable to the Flink community.

Now, let's take a look at what Flink is and how the project came about.

First Look at Apache Flink

The Apache Flink (*http://flink.apache.org/*) project home page starts with the tagline, "Apache Flink is an open source platform for distributed stream and batch data processing." For many people, it's a surprise to realize that Flink not only provides real-time streaming with high throughput and exactly-once guarantees, but it's also an engine for batch data processing. You used to have to choose between these approaches, but Flink lets you do both with one technology.

How did this top-level Apache project get started? Flink has its origins in the Stratosphere project, a research project conducted by three Berlin-based Universities as well as other European Universities between 2010 and 2014. The project had already attracted a broader community base, in part through presentations at several public developer conferences including Berlin Buzzwords, NoSQL Matters in Cologne, and others. This strong community base is one reason the project was appropriate for incubation under the Apache Software Foundation.

A fork of the Stratosphere code was donated in April 2014 to the Apache Software Foundation as an incubating project, with an initial set of committers consisting of the core developers of the system. Shortly thereafter, many of the founding committers left university to start a company to commercialize Flink: data Artisans. During incubation, the project name had to be changed from Stratosphere because of potential confusion with an unrelated project. The name Flink was selected to honor the style of this stream and batch processor: in German, the word "flink" means fast or agile. A logo showing a colorful squirrel was chosen because squirrels are fast, agile and—in the case of squirrels in Berlin—an amazing shade of reddish-brown, as you can see in Figure 1-3.

Figure 1-3. Left: Red squirrel in Berlin with spectacular ears. Right: Apache Flink logo with spectacular tail. Its colors reflect that of the Apache Software Foundation logo. It's an Apache-style squirrel!

The project completed incubation quickly, and in December 2014, Flink graduated to become a top-level project of the Apache Software Foundation. Flink is one of the 5 largest big data projects of the Apache Software Foundation, with a community of more than 200 developers across the globe and several production installations, some in Fortune Global 500 companies. At the time of this writing, 34 Apache Flink meetups take place in cities around the world (*http://www.meetup.com/topics/apache-flink/*), with approximately 12,000 members and Flink speakers participating at big data conferences. In October 2015, the Flink project held its first annual conference in Berlin: Flink Forward.

Batch and Stream Processing

How and why does Flink handle both batch and stream processing? Flink treats batch processing—that is, processing of static and finite data—as a special case of stream processing.

The core computational fabric of Flink, labeled "Flink runtime" in Figure 1-4, is a distributed system that accepts streaming dataflow programs and executes them in a fault-tolerant manner in one or more machines. This runtime can run in a cluster, as an application of YARN (Yet Another Resource Negotiator) or soon in a Mesos cluster (under development), or within a single machine, which is very useful for debugging Flink applications.

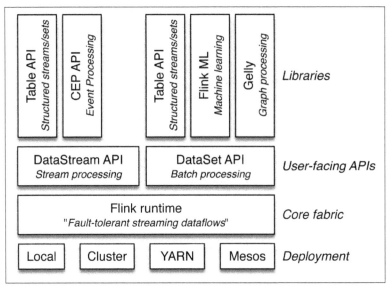

Figure 1-4. This diagram depicts the key components of the Flink stack. Notice that the user-facing layer includes APIs for both stream and batch processing, making Flink a single tool to work with data in either situation. Libraries include machine learning (FlinkML), complex event processing (CEP), and graph processing (Gelly), as well as Table API for stream or batch mode.

Programs accepted by the runtime are very powerful, but are verbose and difficult to program directly. For that reason, Flink offers developer-friendly APIs that layer on top of the runtime and generate these streaming dataflow programs. There is the DataStream API for stream processing and a DataSet API for batch processing. It is interesting to note that, although the runtime of Flink was always based on streams, the DataSet API predates the DataStream API, as the industry need for processing infinite streams was not as widespread in the first Flink years.

The DataStream API is a fluent API for defining analytics on possibly infinite data streams. The API is available in Java or Scala. Users work with a data structure called DataStream, which represents distributed, possibly infinite streams.

Flink is distributed in the sense that it can run on hundreds or thousands of machines, distributing a large computation in small chunks, with each machine executing one chunk. The Flink framework automatically takes care of correctly restoring the computation in the event of machine and other failures, or intentional reprocessing, as in the case of bug fixes or version upgrades. This capability alleviates the need for the programmer to worry about failures. Flink internally uses fault-tolerant streaming data flows, allowing developers to analyze never-ending streams of data that are continuously produced (stream processing).

 Because Flink handles many issues of concern, such as exactly-once guarantees and data windows based in event time, developers no longer need to accommodate these in the application layer. That style leads to fewer bugs.

Teams get the best out of their engineers' time because they aren't burdened by having to take care of problems in their application code. This benefit not only affects development time, it also improves quality through flexibility and makes operations easier to carry out efficiently. Flink provides a robust way for an application to perform well in production. This is not just theory—despite being a relatively new project, Flink software is already being used in production, as we will see in the next section.

Flink in Production

This chapter raises the question, "Why Apache Flink?" One good way to answer that is to hear what people using Flink in production have to say about why they chose it and what they're using it for.

Bouygues Telecom

Bouygues Telecom is the third-largest mobile provider in France and is part of the Bouygues Group, which ranks in Fortune's "Global 500." Bouygues uses Flink for real-time event processing and analytics for billions of messages per day in a system that is running 24/7. In a June 2015 post (*http://data-artisans.com/flink-at-bouygues-html/*) by Mohamed Amine Abdessemed, on the data Artisans blog, a representative from Bouygues described the company's project goals and why it chose Flink to meet them.

> Bouygues "...ended up with Flink because the system supports true streaming—both at the API and at the runtime level, giving us the programmability and low latency that we were looking for. In addition, we were able to get our system up and running with Flink in a

fraction of the time compared to other solutions, which resulted in more available developer resources for expanding the business logic in the system."

This work was also reported at the Flink Forward conference (*http:// bit.ly/2avmEhL*) in October 2015. Bouygues wanted to give its engineers real-time insights about customer experience, what is happening globally on the network, and what is happening in terms of network evolutions and operations.

To do this, its team built a system to analyze network equipment logs to identify indicators of the quality of user experience. The system handles 2 billion events per day (500,000 events per second) with a required end-to-end latency of less than 200 milliseconds (including message publication by the transport layer and data processing in Flink). This was achieved on a small cluster reported to be only 10 nodes with 1 gigabyte of memory each. Bouygues also wanted other groups to be able to reuse partially processed data for a variety of business intelligence (BI) purposes, without interfering with one another.

The company's plan was to use Flink's stream processing to transform and enrich data. The derived stream data would then be pushed back to the message transport system to make this data available for analytics by multiple consumers.

This approach was chosen explicitly *instead of* other design options, such as processing the data before it enters the message queue, or delegating the processing to multiple applications that consume from the message queue.

Flink's stream processing capability allowed the Bouygues team to complete the data processing and movement pipeline while meeting the latency requirement and with high reliability, high availability, and ease of use. The Flink framework, for instance, is ideal for debugging, and it can be switched to local execution. Flink also supports program visualization to help understand how programs are running. Furthermore, the Flink APIs are attractive to both developers and data scientists. In Mohamed Amine Abdessemed's blog post, Bouygues reported interest in Flink by other teams for different use cases.

Other Examples of Apache Flink in Production

King.com

It's a pretty fair assumption that right now someone, in some place in the world, is playing a King game online. This leading online entertainment company states that it has developed more than 200 games, offered in more than 200 countries and regions.

As the King engineers describe (*https://techblog.king.com/rbea-scalable-real-time-analytics-king/*): "With over 300 million monthly unique users and over 30 billion events received every day from the different games and systems, any stream analytics use case becomes a real technical challenge. It is crucial for our business to develop tools for our data analysts that can handle these massive data streams while keeping maximal flexibility for their applications."

The system that the company built using Apache Flink allows data scientists at King to get access in these massive data streams in real time. They state that they are impressed by Apache Flink's level of maturity. Even with such a complex application as this online game case, Flink is able to address the solution almost out of the box.

Zalando

As a leading online fashion platform in Europe, Zalando has more than 16 million customers worldwide. On its website, it describes the company as working with "...small, agile, autonomous teams" (another way to say this is that they employ a microservices style of architecture).

A stream-based architecture nicely supports a microservices approach, and Flink provides stream processing that is needed for this type of work, in particular for business process monitoring and continuous Extract, Transform and Load (ETL) in Zalando's use case (*https://tech.zalando.de/blog/apache-showdown-flink-vs.-spark/*).

Otto Group

The Otto Group is the world's second-largest online retailer in the end-consumer (B2C) business, and Europe's largest online retailer in the B2C fashion and lifestyle business.

The BI department of the Otto Group had resorted to developing its own streaming engine, because when it first evaluated the open source options, it could not find one that fit its requirements. After testing Flink, the department found it fit their needs for stream processing, which include crowd-sourced user-agent identification, and a search session identifier.

ResearchGate

ResearchGate is the largest academic social network in terms of active users. ResearchGate has adopted Flink in production since 2014, using it as one of its primary tools in the data infrastructure for both batch and stream processing.

Alibaba Group

This huge ecommerce group works with buyers and suppliers via its web portal. The company's online recommendations are produced by a variation of Flink (called Blink). One of the attractions of working with a true streaming engine such as Flink is that purchases that are being made during the day can be taken into account when recommending products to users. This is particularly important on special days (holidays) when the activity is unusually high. This is an example of a use case where efficient stream processing is a big advantage over batch processing.

Where Flink Fits

We began this chapter with the question, "Why Flink?" A larger question, of course, is, "Why work with streaming data?" We've touched on the answer to that—many of the situations we want to observe and analyze involve data from continuous events. Rather than being something special, streaming data is in many situations what is natural—it's just that in the past we've had to devise clever compromises to work with it in a somewhat artificial way, as batches, in order to meet the demands posed by handling data and computation at very large scale. It's not that working with streaming data is entirely new; it's that we have new technologies that enable us to do this at larger scale, more flexibly, and in a natural and more affordable way than before.

Flink isn't the only technology available to work with stream processing. There are a number of emerging technologies being developed and improved to address these needs. Obviously people choose to work with a particular technology for a variety of reasons, including existing expertise within their teams. But the strengths of Flink, the ease of working with it, and the wide range of ways it can be used to advantage make it an attractive option. That along with a growing and energetic community says that it is probably worth examination. You may find that the answer to "Why Flink?" turns out to be, "Why *not* Flink?"

Before we look in more detail at how Flink works, in Chapter 2 we will explore how to design data architecture to get the best advantage from stream processing and, indeed, how a stream-first architecture provides more far-reaching benefits.

Stream-First Architecture

There is a revolution underway in how people design their data architecture, not just for real-time or near real–time projects, but in a larger sense as well. The change is to think of stream-based data flow as the heart of the overall design, rather than the basis just for specialized work. Understanding the motivations for this transformation to a stream-first architecture helps put Apache Flink and its role in modern data processing into context.

Flink, as part of a newer breed of systems, does its part to broaden the scope of the term "data streaming" way beyond real-time, low-latency analytics to encompass a wide variety of data applications, including what is now covered by stream processors, what is covered by batch processors, and even some stateful applications that are executed by transactional databases.

As it turns out, the data architecture needed to put Flink to work effectively is also the basis for gaining broader advantages from working with streaming data. To understand how this works, we will take a closer look at how to build the pipeline to support Flink for stream processing. But first, let's address the question of what is to be gained from working with a stream-focused architecture instead of the more traditional approach.

Traditional Architecture versus Streaming Architecture

Traditionally, the typical architecture of a data backend has employed a centralized database system to hold the transactional data of the business. In other words, the database (be that a SQL or NoSQL database) holds the "fresh" (another word for "accurate") data, which represents the state of the business *right now*. This might, for example, mean how many users are logged in to your system, how many active users a website has, or what the current balance of each user account is. Data applications that need fresh data are implemented against the database. Other data stores such as distributed file systems are used for data that need not be updated frequently and for which very large batch computations are needed.

This traditional architecture has served applications well for decades, but is now being strained under the burden of increasing complexity in very large-scale distributed systems. Some of the main problems that companies have observed are:

- The pipeline from data ingestion to analytics is too complex and slow for many projects.
- The traditional architecture is too monolithic: the database backend acts as a single source of truth, and all applications need to access this backend for their data needs.
- Systems built this way have very complex failure modes that can make it hard to keep them running well.

Another problem of this traditional architecture stems from trying to maintain the current "state of the world" consistently across a large, distributed system. At scale, it becomes harder and harder to maintain such precise synchronization; stream-first architectures allow us to relax the requirements so that we only need to maintain much more localized consistency.

A modern alternative approach, *streaming architecture*, solves many of the problems that enterprises face when working with large-scale systems. In a stream-based design, we take this a step further and let data records continuously flow from data sources to applications and between applications. There is no single database that holds the global state of the world. Rather, the single source of truth is in shared, ever-moving event streams—this is what represents the *his-*

tory of the business. In this stream-first architecture, applications themselves build their local views of the world, stored in local databases, distributed files, or search documents, for instance.

Message Transport and Message Processing

What is needed to implement an effective stream-first architecture and to gain the advantages of using Flink? A common pattern is to implement a streaming architecture by using two main kinds of components, described briefly here and represented in Figure 2-1:

1. **A message transport** to collect and deliver data from continuous events from a variety of sources (producers) and make this data available to applications and services that subscribe to it (consumers).

2. **A stream processing system** to (1) consistently move data between applications and systems, (2) aggregate and process events, and (3) maintain local application state (again consistently).

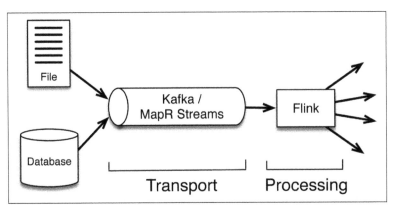

Figure 2-1. Flink projects have two main components of the architecture: the transport stage for delivery of messages from continuous events and the processing stage, which Flink provides. Messaging technologies with the needed capabilities include Apache Kafka and MapR Streams, which is compatible with the Kafka API and is an integral part of the MapR converged data platform.

The excitement around real-time applications tends to direct people's attention to component number 2 in our list, the stream processing system, and how to choose a technology for stream processing that can meet the requirements of a particular project. In addition to using Flink for data processing, there are other choices that you can employ (e.g., Spark Streaming, Storm, Samza, Apex). We use Apache Flink as the stream processor in the rest of the examples in this book.

As it turns out, it isn't just the choice of the stream processor that makes a big difference to designing an efficient stream-based architecture. The transport layer is also key. A big part of why modern systems can more easily handle streaming data at large scale is improvements in the way message-passing systems work and changes to how the processing elements interact with those systems.

The message transport layer needs to have certain capabilities to make streaming design work well. At present, two messaging technologies offer a particularly good fit to the required capabilities: Kafka and MapR Streams, which supports the Kafka API but is built into the MapR converged data platform. In this book, we assume that one or the other of these technologies provide the transport layer in our examples.

The Transport Layer: Ideal Capabilities

What are the capabilities needed by the message transport system in streaming architecture?

Performance with Persistence

One of the roles of the transport layer is to serve as a safety queue upstream from the processing step—a buffer to hold event data as a kind of short-term insurance against an interruption in processing as data is ingested. Until recently, message-passing technologies were limited by a tradeoff between performance and persistence. As a result, people tended to think of streaming data going from the transport layer to processing and then being discarded: a use it and lose it approach.

The assumption that you can't have both performance and persistence is one of key ideas that has changed in order to design a modern streaming architecture. It's important to have a message transport that delivers high throughput *with* persistence; both Kafka and MapR's MapR Streams do just that.

A key benefit of a persistent transport layer is that *messages are replayable*. This key capability allows a data processor like Flink to replay and recompute a specified part of the stream of events (discussed in further detail in Chapter 5). For now, the key is to recognize that it is the interplay of transport and processing that allows a system like Flink to provide guarantees about correct processing and to do "time travel," which refers to the ability to reprocess data.

Decoupling of Multiple Producers from Multiple Consumers

An effective messaging technology enables collection of data from many sources (producers) and makes it available to multiple services or applications (consumers), as depicted in Figure 2-2. With Kafka and MapR Streams, data from producers is assigned to a named topic. Data sources push data to the message queue, and consumers (or consumer groups) pull data. Event data can only be read forward from a given offset in the message queue. Producers do not broadcast to all consumers automatically. This may sound like a small detail, but this characteristic has an enormous impact on how this architecture functions.

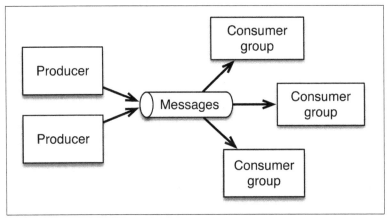

Figure 2-2. With message-transport tools such as Kafka and MapR Streams, data producers and data consumers (of which Flink applications would be included) are decoupled. Messages arrive ready for immediate use or to be consumed later. Consumers subscribe to messages from the queue instead of messages being broadcast. A consumer need not be running at the time a message arrives.

This style of delivery—with consumers subscribing to their topics of interest—means that messages arrive immediately, *but they don't need to be processed immediately.* Consumers don't need to be running when the messages arrive; they can make use of the data any time they like. New consumers or producers can also be added easily. Having a message-transport system that decouples producers from consumers is powerful because it can support a *microservices approach* and allows processing steps to hide their implementations, and thus provides them with the freedom to change those implementations.

Streaming Data for a Microservices Architecture

A microservices approach refers to breaking functions in large systems into simple, generally single-purpose services that can be built and maintained easily by small teams. This design enables agility even in very large organizations. To work properly, the connections that communicate between services need to be lightweight.

"The goal [of microservices] is to give each team a job and a way to do it and to get out of their way."

From Chapter 3 of *Streaming Architecture*, Dunning and Friedman (O'Reilly, 2016)

Using a message-transport system that decouples producers and consumers but delivers messages with high throughput, sufficient for high-performance processors such as Flink, is a great way to build a microservices organization. Streaming data is a relatively new way to connect microservices, but it has considerable benefits, as you'll see in the next couple of sections.

Data Stream as the Centralized Source of Data

Now you can put together these ideas to envision how message-transport queues interconnect various applications to become, essentially, the heart of the streaming architecture. The stream processor (Flink, in our case) subscribes to data from the message queues and processes it. The output can go to another message-transport queue. That way other applications, including other Flink applications, have access to the shared streaming data. In some cases, the output is stored in a local database. This approach is depicted in Figure 2-3.

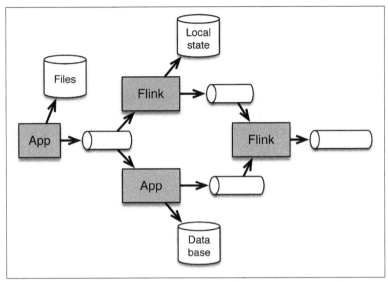

Figure 2-3. In a stream-first architecture, the message stream (repre-sented here as blank horizontal cylinder) connects applications and serves as the new shared source of truth, taking the role that a huge centralized database used to do. In our example, Flink is used for vari-ous applications. Localized views can be stored in files or databases as needed for the requirements of microservices-based projects. An added advantage to this streaming style of architecture is that the stream pro-cessor, such as Flink, can help maintain consistency.

> In the streaming architecture, there need not be a centralized database. Instead, the message queues serve as a shared information source for a variety of different consumers.

Fraud Detection Use Case: Better Design with Stream-First Architecture

The power of the stream-based microservices architecture is seen in the flexibility it adds, especially when the same data is used in multi-ple ways. Take the example of a fraud-detection project for a credit card provider. The goal is to identify suspicious card behavior as quickly as possible in order to shut down a potential theft with mini-mal losses. The fraud detector might, for example, use card velocity as one indicator of potential fraud: do sequential transactions take place across too great a distance in too short a time to be legiti-mately possible? A real fraud detector will use many dozens or hun-dreds of such features, but we can understand a lot by dealing with just this one.

The advantages of stream-based architecture for this use case are shown in Figure 2-4. In this figure, many point-of-sale terminals (POS1 through POSn) ask the fraud detector to make fraud deci-sions. These requests from the point-of-sale terminals need to be answered immediately and form a call-and-response kind of inter-action with the fraud detector.

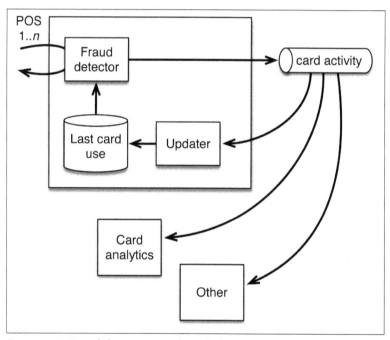

Figure 2-4. Fraud detection can benefit from a stream-based microser-vices approach. Flink would be useful in several components of this data flow: the fraud-detector application, the updater, and even the card analytics could all use Flink. Notice that by avoiding direct updates to a local database, streaming data for card activity can be used by other services, including card analytics without interference. [Image credit: Streaming Architecture, Chapter 6, (O'Reilly, 2016).]

In a traditional system, the fraud-detection model would store a profile containing the last location for each credit card directly in the database. But in such a centralized database design, other consumers cannot easily make use of the card activity data due to the risk that their access might interfere with the essential function of the fraud-detection system, and they certainly wouldn't be allowed to make changes to the schema or technology of that database without very careful and arduous review. The result is a huge slowing of progress resulting from all of the due diligence that must be applied to avoid breaking or compromising business-critical functions.

Compare that traditional approach to the streaming design illustrated in Figure 2-4. By sending the output of the fraud detector to an external message-transport queue (Kafka or MapR Streams) instead of directly to the database and then using a stream processor such as Flink to update the database, the card activity data becomes available to other applications such as card analytics via the message queue. The database of last card use becomes a completely local source of information, inaccessible to any other service. This design avoids any risk of overload due to additional applications.

Flexibility for Developers

This stream-based microservices architecture also provides flexibility for developers of the fraud-detection system. Suppose that this team wants to develop and evaluate an improved model for fraud detection? The card activity message stream makes this data available for the new system without interfering with the existing detector. Additional readers of the queue impose almost negligible load on the queue, and each additional service is free to keep historical information in any format or database technology that is appropriate. Moreover, if the messages in the card activity queue are expressed as business-level events rather than, say, database table updates, the exact form and content of the messages will tend to be very stable. When changes are necessary, they can often be forward-compatible to avoid changes to existing applications.

This credit card fraud detection use case is just one example of the way a stream-based architecture with a proper message transport (Kafka or MapR Streams) and a versatile and highly performant stream processor (Flink) can support a variety of different projects from a shared "source of truth": the message stream.

Beyond Real-Time Applications

As important as they are, low-latency use cases are just one class of consumers for streaming data. Consider various ways that streaming data can be used: Stream-processing applications might, for example, subscribe to streaming data in a message queue, to update a real-time dashboard (see the Group A consumers in Figure 2-5).

Other users could take advantage of the fact that persisted messages can be replayed (see the Group C consumers in Figure 2-5). In this case, the message stream acts as an auditable log or long-term history of events. Having a replayable history is useful, for example, for security analytics, as a part of the input data for predictive mainte-nance models in industrial settings, or for retrospective studies as in medical or environmental research.

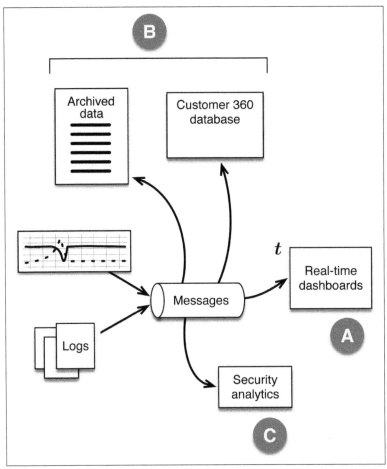

Figure 2-5. The consumers of streaming data are not limited to just low-latency applications, although they are important examples. This diagram illustrates several of the classes of consumers that benefit from a streaming architecture. Group A consumers might be doing various types of real-time analytics, including updating a real-time dashboard. Group B consumers include various local representations of the current state of some aspect of the data, perhaps stored in a database or search document.

For other uses, the data queue is tapped for applications that update a local database or search document (see the Group B use cases in Figure 2-5). Data from the queue is not output directly to a database, by the way. Instead, it must be aggregated or otherwise analyzed and transformed by the stream processor first. This is another situation in which Flink can be used to advantage.

Geo-Distributed Replication of Streams

Stream processing and a stream-first architecture are not experimental toys: these approaches are used in mission-critical applications, and these applications need certain features from both the stream processor and the message transport layer. A wide variety of these critical business uses depend on consistency across data centers, and as such, they not only require a highly effective stream processor, but also message transport with reliable geo-distributed replication. Telecoms, for example, need to share data between cell towers, users, and processing centers. Financial institutions need to be able to replicate data quickly, accurately, and affordably across distant offices. There are many other examples where it's particularly useful if this geo-distribution of data can be done with streaming data.

In particular, to be most useful, this replication between data centers needs to preserve message offsets to allow updates from any of the data centers to be propagated to any of the other data centers and allow bidirectional and cyclic replication of data. If message offsets are not preserved, programs cannot be restarted reliably in another data center. If updates are not allowed from any data center, some sort of master must be designed reliably. And cyclic replication is necessary to avoid single point of failure in replication.

These capabilities are currently supported in the MapR Streams messaging system, but not in Kafka as of yet. The basic idea with MapR Streams transport is that many streaming topics are collected into first-class data structures known as streams that coexist with files, tables, and directories in the MapR data platform. These streams are then the basis for managing replication as well as time-to-live and access control permissions (ACEs). Changes made to topics in a stream are tagged with the source cluster ID to avoid infinite cyclic replication, and these changes are propagated successively to other clusters while maintaining all message offsets.

This ability to replicate streams across data centers extends the usefulness of streaming data and stream processing. Take, for example, a business that serves online ads. Streaming data analysis can be useful in such a business in multiple ways. If you think in terms of the use classes described previously in Figure 2-5, in ad-tech, the real-time applications (Group A) might involve up-to-date inventory control, the current-state view in a database (Group B) might be cookie profiles, and replaying the stream (Group C) would be useful in models to detect clickstream fraud.

In addition to these considerations, there's the challenge that different data centers are handling different bids for the same ads, but they are all drawing from the same pool of ad inventory. In a business where accuracy and speed are important, how do the different centers coordinate availability of inventory? With the message stream as the centrally shared "source of truth," it's particularly powerful in this use case to be able to replicate the stream across different data centers, which MapR Streams can do. This situation is shown in Figure 2-6.

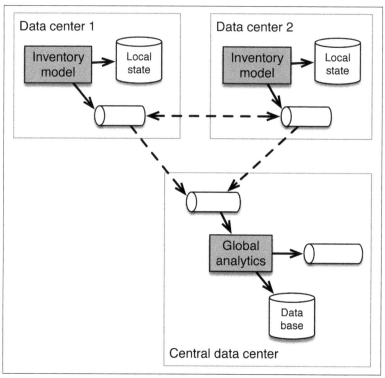

Figure 2-6. Ad-tech industry example analyzes streaming data in different data centers with various model-based applications for which Flink could be useful. Each local data center needs to keep its own current state of transactions, but they are all drawing from a common inventory. Another requirement is to share data with a central data center where Flink could be used for global analytics. This use case calls for efficient and accurate geo-distributed replication, something that can be done with the messaging system MapR Streams, but not currently with Kafka.

In addition to keeping the different parts of the business up to date with regard to shared inventory (a situation that would apply to many other sectors as well), the ability to replicate data streams across data centers has other advantages. Having more than one data center helps spread the load for high volume and decreases propagation delay by moving computation close to end users during bidding and ad placement. Multiple data centers also serve as backups in case of disaster.

In the first two chapters, we've seen that handling and processing data as streams is a good fit for the way data from continuous events naturally occurs. We've also explored the advantages of a stream-based architecture that combines effective message-transport technology, such as Kafka or MapR Streams, with Apache Flink as the stream processor.

In the next chapter, we will examine the key features of Flink and provide an overview of what Flink can do before diving deeper in later chapters into how Flink functions.

CHAPTER 3

What Flink Does

Apache Flink brings a fresh approach to the role of stream processor, completing the streaming architecture described in Chapter 2. One of the strengths of a technology like this is the way it lets you build applications that are a good fit for real life. In order to understand what Flink does and how you might want to use it, consider here some of the key aspects of what makes it versatile, and in particular what makes it able to address "correctness" in several important ways.

Different Types of Correctness

In Chapter 1, we saw the consequences of not doing streaming well. Here, we look at how Flink helps do streaming correctly and what this means. In the simplest sense, people think of correctness as accuracy—if you are counting, for example, have you counted correctly? That's a good point, but there are really a number of issues that affect "correct," especially if you think of it in the slightly larger terms of how well your computation fits the world you are trying to model and analyze. Another way to put this is: for your data processing, you want "what you want, what you expect, when you want it."

Natural Fit for Sessions

One way in which streaming in general and Flink in particular offers correctness is through a more natural fit between the way computational windows are defined and how data naturally occurs. Think of the situation of tracking the activity of three users (A, B, and C in Figure 3-1) on a website monitored through clickstream data. For each user, web activity is sporadic. There are periods of website activity in which event data is collected, separated by periods with a gap in data, when the user goes off for a cup of coffee or switches back to their workscreen when their manager walks by. How well does your processing framework enable you to fit your computational window for web activity analytics to the actual behavior of the users? In other words, what's the match between naturally occurring web sessions and your computational window?

First let's look at what happens in this example when the analysis of web behavior is done with micro-batching or fixed computational windows, as depicted in Figure 3-1.

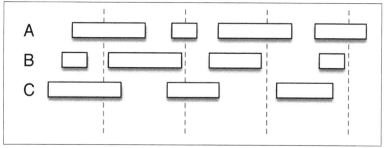

Figure 3-1. With micro-batching, it's difficult to define computation windows (marked by dashed lines) such that they do not overlap naturally occurring sessions of activity (shown here as rectangles) for the users A, B, and C.

The micro-batch window is an externally defined interval that may make it difficult to align with actual sessions of activity. The situation is different when you can define windows more flexibly, as you can do in Flink's stream processing API. A developer can, for example, use a configurable threshold of inactivity to mark the end of a session—perhaps, say, every time there is a gap of more than five minutes, close a session. This style of windowing is shown in Figure 3-2.

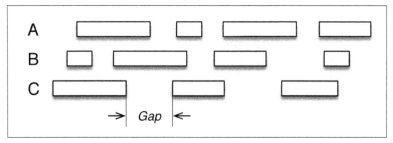

Figure 3-2. Flink's stream processing lets you define windows such that they have a better fit to how sessions naturally occur. Here the diagram indicates that windows can be triggered by a defined gap between sessions of activity. In this example, all of these sessions had a gap between the time of sequential events greater than the defined threshold, hence marking the end of each session.

The key idea here is that Flink can denote computational windows that reflect actual sessions of activity.

Event Time versus Processing Time

As a side note, there's more than one way to designate time as you program. For the purpose of assigning events to a particular session window, such as the case depicted in Figure 3-2, it's likely the developer would have chosen *event time*, which is the time clock that is based on when an event actually happened. Another approach is to use *processing time*, which reflects an internal clock in the system and denotes a particular point at which a streaming event is handled by the program. The notions of time, what they mean in terms of working with Flink, and details of windowing are explained in depth in Chapter 4.

Event Time

It's generally unusual for streaming frameworks to handle event time, although this is gaining a lot of popularity. Flink can do so, which is powerful in terms of correctness of calculations. For best results, you want to have the option of a clock for your system that can look at the data to figure out what time events occurred, rather than only being able to use an internal clock (processing time).

The greater accuracy this choice allows was demonstrated recently at an OSCON workshop presented by Jamie Grier (*http://bit.ly/2bho7Fl*). He generated data to simulate sensor measurements of pressure and wrote a Flink program to compute the sum of sine waves over a one-second interval for sine waves with a total period of one second. The correct answer should be zero. He compared what happens when the computation is done over windows defined by processing time or when event time is used. With processing time, there was lots of noise around the correct response of zero, but when he switched to defining computation windows by event time, the results smoothed out to an accurate "zero" as the consistent response. This comparison is shown in Figure 3-3.

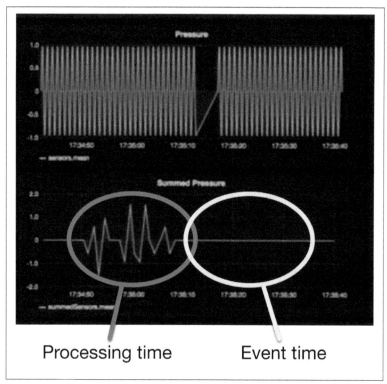

Figure 3-3. Switching from using processing time to using event time makes many computations work better. Using processing time (red circle) on data that should sum to zero results in errors. Using event time instead (yellow circle) results in correct results. (From demonstration by Jamie Grier at OSCON (http://bit.ly/2bho7Fl), May 2016.)

The separation of different types of time in Flink is part of what makes it able to do more than older streaming systems.

Accuracy Under Failures: Keeping Track of State

To maintain accuracy, a computation must keep track of state. If it's not done by the computational framework, the task falls to the developer and application to do it. To do this is especially hard with continuous stream processing—there's no end point at which you stop and tally up. Instead, you have to keep updating state as you go.

Flink has addressed several of the issues that could potentially impair correctness, including stateful computations even after a failure.

The underlying technology that Flink uses to address this challenge is called *checkpoints*, and how this works is described in detail in Chapter 5. Checkpoints enable fault tolerance by keeping track of intermediate conditions of state such that the system can be accurately reset if there is a failure. And it does this with relatively low and configurable overhead. Flink's approach has very little impact when the system is running smoothly (without failing).

Keep in mind that checkpoints are also what support Flink's ability to reprocess data when you choose to do so, not just in the case of a failure. For example, you may want to replay and reprocess the steam of event data because you want to run a new model or do a bug fix. Flink makes this possible.

Flink's checkpoint feature that enables it to accurately maintain state and reprocess data efficiently is unique among stream processors.

Answers When They Matter

It may seem surprising to include Flink's capability for very low-latency applications in the idea of "correctness." Think of it this way: some answers may be accurate, such as a sum or average, but if they aren't achieved fast enough to meet your needs, it's hard to think of the results as being correct. To get the idea, think about a crowd-sourced traffic and navigation application for smartphones. If you as a driver are on your way to work and you want to know which of two major freeways is less congested, it's not much of a help if your application calculates an accurate assessment of traffic conditions for your commute but provides the results *two hours after your drive*. Even a five-second delay *after* you have taken the wrong turn at an intersection would be problematic.

There are real situations where very low latency truly matters so that the system can return results on demand, and not only when they have been computed to completion. Flink's ability to provide real-time, fault-tolerant stream processing addresses that aspect of correctness.

Ease of Development and Operations

A final way in which Flink's design contributes to overall correctness is in its human interface. Flink's expressivity makes the developer's job easier, and that in turn makes it less likely for mistakes to occur and persist. In addition, the fact that the Flink framework takes the burden of maintaining state, which would otherwise be up to the developer to build into the application, also makes programming easier and the application more likely to succeed. Being able to use one technology for stream processing as well as for batch jobs also simplifies both development and operations.

Hierarchical Use Cases: Adopting Flink in Stages

While Flink offers a wide range of capabilities, including some very sophisticated ways of handling data, it's not necessary to plunge into it all at once. The move to a stream-first architecture can be done in steps. We see some enterprises adopting streaming by first implementing simple applications in a streaming architecture and then moving on to other applications. Although the type of applications depend highly on the company's needs, we have observed a typical "value chain" of streaming use cases that many companies move up to.

Now, take the opportunity to dive in deeper into what Flink does, and *how* it does it; many of its fundamental capabilities are explained in Chapters 4–6.

CHAPTER 4

Handling Time

One crucial difference between programming applications for a stream processor and a batch processor is the need to explicitly handle time. Let us take a very simple application: counting. We have a never-ending stream of events coming in (e.g., tweets, clicks, transactions), and we want to group the events by a key, and periodically (say, every hour) output the count of the distinct events for each key. This is the proverbial application for "big data" that is analogous to the infamous word-counting example for MapReduce.

Counting with Batch and Lambda Architectures

Even if this seems simple, counting is surprisingly difficult at scale and in practice, and, of course, appears everywhere. Other analytics, such as aggregations or operations on Online Analytical Processing (OLAP) cubes, are simple generalizations of counting. Using a traditional batch-processing architecture, we would implement this as shown in Figure 4-1.

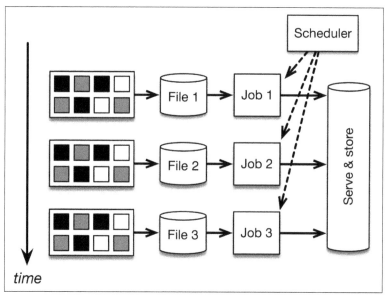

Figure 4-1. Implementing continuous applications using periodic batch jobs. Data is continuously sliced into files, possibly on an hourly basis, and batch jobs are run with these files as input, giving an impression of a continuous processing of incoming data.

In this architecture, a continuous data ingestion pipeline creates files (typically stored in a distributed file store such as Hadoop Distributed File System [HDFS] or MapR-FS) every hour. This can be done by using a tool like Apache Flume. A batch job (using MapReduce or some alternative) is scheduled by a scheduler to analyze the last file produced—grouping the events in the file *by key*, and counting distinct events per key—to output the last counts. Every company that is using Hadoop has several pipelines like this running in their clusters.

Although this architecture can certainly be made to work, there are several problems with it:

- *Too many moving parts:* We are using a lot of systems to count events in our incoming data. All of these come with their learning and administration costs as well as bugs in all of the different programs.

- *Implicit treatment of time:* Let's assume that we want to count every 30 minutes rather than every hour. This logic is part of the workflow scheduling (and not the application code) logic, which mixes DevOps concerns with business requirements.

- *Early alerts:* Let's say that we want to get early count alerts as soon as possible (when receiving, say, at least 10 events), in addition to counting every one hour. For that, we can use Storm to ingest the message stream (Kafka or MapR Streams) in addition to the periodic batch jobs. Storm provides early approximate counts, and the periodic jobs provide the accurate hourly counts. We just added yet another system to the mix, along with a new programming model. This is called the Lambda architecture, described briefly in Chapter 1 and shown here in Figure 4-2.

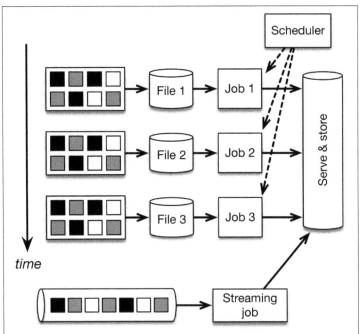

Figure 4-2. Implementing continuous applications using periodic batch jobs and early results using a stream processor (Lambda architecture). The stream processor is used to provide approximate but real-time results, which are eventually corrected by the batch layer.

- *Out of order events:* In most real-world streams, events can arrive out of order; that is, the order that the events occur in the real world (as indicated by the timestamps attached to the events when they are produced [e.g., the time measured by the smartphone when a user logs in an application]) is different from the order in which the events are observed in the data center. This means that an event that belongs to the previous hourly batch may be wrongly counted in the current batch. There is really no straightforward way to resolve this using this architecture—most people choose simply to ignore that this reality exists.

- *Unclear batch boundaries*: The meaning of "hourly" is kind of ambiguous in this architecture, as it really depends on the interaction between different systems. The hourly batches are, at best, approximate, with events at the edges of batches ending up in either the current or the next batch, with few guarantees. Cutting the data stream into hourly batches is actually the simplest possible way to divide time. Assume that we would like to produce aggregates, not for simple hourly batches, but instead for sessions of activity (e.g., from login until logout or inactivity). There is no straightforward way to do this with the architecture shown in Figure 4-1 and Figure 4-2.

Counting with Streaming Architecture

There surely must be a better way to produce counts from a stream of events. As you might have suspected already, this is a streaming use case in which we use periodic batch jobs to simulate streaming. In addition, we must glue together a variety of systems. Using a streaming architecture, the application would follow the model in Figure 4-3.

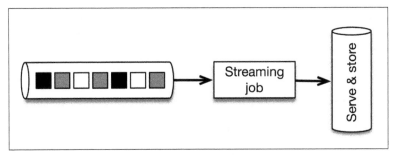

Figure 4-3. Implementing continuous applications using a streaming architecture. The message transport (Kafka, MapR Streams) is shown here as a horizontal cylinder. It supplies streaming data to the stream processor (in our case, Flink) that is used for all data processing, providing both real-time results and correct results.

The event stream is again served by the message transport and simply consumed by a single Flink job that produces hourly counts and (optional) early alerts. This approach solves all the previous problems in a straightforward way. Slowdowns in the Flink job or throughput spikes simply pile up in the message-transport tool. The logic to divide events into timely batches (called *windows*) is embedded entirely in the application logic of the Flink program. Early alerts are produced by the same program. Out-of-order events are transparently handled by Flink. Grouping by session instead of a fixed time means simply changing the window definition in the Flink program. Additionally, replaying the application with changed code means simply replaying the Kafka topic. By adopting a streaming architecture, we have vastly reduced the number of systems to learn, administer, and create code in. The Flink application code to do this counting is straightforward:

```
DataStream<LogEvent> stream = env
  // create stream from Kafka
  .addSource(new FlinkKafkaConsumer(...))
  // group by country
  .keyBy("country")
  // window of size 1 hour
  .timeWindow(Time.minutes(60))
  // do operations per window
  .apply(new CountPerWindowFunction());
```

There are two main differences between the two approaches: 1) we are treating the never-ending stream of incoming events as what it actually is—a stream—rather than trying to artificially cut it into files, and 2) we are explicitly encoding the definition of time (to divide the stream into groups) in the application code (the time window above) instead of implicitly spreading its definition to ingestion, computation, and scheduling.

Batching in Stream Processing Systems

The term "micro-batching," as we discussed in Chapter 1, has been used to refer to something in between batch and streaming. In reality, micro-batching can mean widely different things depending on the context. In some sense, the batch architecture we saw in Figure 4-1 is a micro-batch architecture if the files are sufficiently small.

Storm Trident implements micro-batching by creating a large Storm event that contains a fixed number of events and processing the aggregated events with a continuously running Storm topology. Spark Streaming implements micro-batching as essentially the batch architecture we saw, but hiding the first two steps (ingestion and storage) from the user and storing the mini-batches internally in memory, in a write-ahead log instead of in files. Finally, every modern stream processor, including Flink, uses a form of micro-batches internally by sending buffers that contain many events over the network in shuffle phases instead of individual events. All of these forms of micro-batching are widely different.

To be clear, batching in stream processing systems should satisfy the following requirements:

- Batching should be used only as a mechanism to improve performance. The larger the batches, the larger the throughput a system can scale to.

- Batching for performance should be completely independent of buffering for defining windows, or commits for fault tolerance, and should not be part of the API. Coupling these leads to systems that are limited, hard to use, and fragile.

In the end, as an application developer and user of data processing systems, you should not be concerned about whether a system implements micro-batching and how. Instead, you should worry about whether the system can handle out-of-order streams and sessions and other misaligned windows, whether it can provide early alerts in addition to accurate aggregates, and whether it can deter-

ministically replay past data, as well as the performance characteris-
tics of the system (latency and throughput) and the guarantees of
the system in cases of failures.

Notions of Time

In stream processing, we generally speak about two main notions of
time:[1]

- *Event time* is the time that an event actually happened in the real
  world. More accurately, each event is usually associated with a
  timestamp that is part of the data record itself (e.g., as measured
  by a mobile phone or a server that emits logs). The event time
  of an event is simply a timestamp.

- *Processing time* is the time that the event is observed by the
  machine that is processing it. The processing time of an event is
  simply the time measured by the clock of the machine that is
  processing the event.

Figure 4-4 illustrates the difference between event time and processing time.

---

1 Many of the ideas in this chapter were pioneered by the work of the Google Dataflow
team (now Apache Beam [incubating]), including Tyler Akidau, Frances Perry, and
others. Tyler Akidau's articles Streaming 101 (*https://www.oreilly.com/ideas/the-world-
beyond-batch-streaming-101*) and Streaming 102 (*https://www.oreilly.com/ideas/the-
world-beyond-batch-streaming-102*) are excellent reads if you'd like to dig further into
the Dataflow model. Flink's mechanisms for handling time and windows are in large
part rooted in the broad concepts of the Dataflow paper (*http://www.vldb.org/pvldb/
vol8/p1792-Akidau.pdf*) in VLDB 2015.

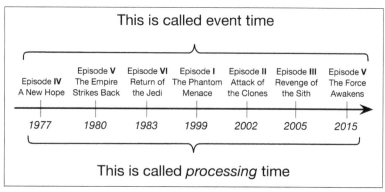

Figure 4-4. An example of an out-of-order stream of events where processing time order is different from event time order.

Consider the *Star Wars* series of movies: the first movies that appeared in the theaters in 1977, 1980, and 1983 (this is the processing time) were movies 4, 5, and 6 in the plot of the series (which is the event time). Then, the movies that appeared in 1999, 2002, 2005, and 2015 in processing time refer to movies 1, 2, 3, and 7 in event time. Hence, streams can arrive out of order (although typically not years out of order).

Often, a third notion of time called *ingestion time* or *ingress time* is used, referring to the time that the event enters the stream processing framework. Data that lacks a true event time may be assigned a time, but these timestamps are simply assigned by the stream processor when it first sees the event (in the source function, the first operator of the program).

Due to various real-world factors (e.g., temporary lack of connectivity, varying delays of the network, clocks in distributed systems, data rate spikes, physics, or just bad luck), event time and processing time always have a time-varying lag (called *event time skew*). The order of events based on event time is often not the same as the order based on processing time; that is, events arrive at the stream processor out of order.

Both notions of time are useful depending on the application. Some applications (e.g., some alerting applications) need results as fast as possible and are happy if these results are slightly inaccurate. In such cases, it is not necessary to wait for late events, and processing time semantics is a great choice. Other applications (e.g., fraud detection or billing) need accuracy: an event should be accounted for in the time window that it actually happened. For these applications, event time semantics is usually the right choice. And there are also applications that need both, perhaps to produce accurate counts, but also to provide an early alert if an anomaly is detected.

 Flink allows the user to define windows in processing time, ingestion time, or event time, depending on the desired semantics and accuracy needs of the application.

When a window is defined in event time, the application can handle out-of-order events and varying event-time skew. It will compute meaningful results with respect to the time inherent to the events.

Windows

In the first section of this chapter, we reviewed an example of defining a time window in Flink, to aggregate the results of the last hour. *Windows* are the mechanism to group and collect a bunch of events by time or some other characteristic in order to do some analysis on these events as a whole (e.g., to sum them up).

Time Windows

The simplest and most useful form of windows are those based on time. Time windows can be *tumbling* or *sliding*. For example, assume that we are counting the values emitted by a sensor and compare these choices:

A tumbling window of 1 minute collects the values of the last minute, and emits their sum at the end of the minute, as shown in Figure 4-5.

Input →	9, 6, 8, 4, 7, 3, 8, 4, 2, 1, 3, 2		
Tumbling windows →	9, 6, 8, 4,	7, 3, 8, 4,	2, 1, 3, 2
Output →	27	22	8

Figure 4-5. A tumbling time window of 1 minute that sums the last minute's worth of values.

A sliding window of 1 minute that slides every half minute counts the values of the last minute, emitting the count every half minute, as shown in Figure 4-6.

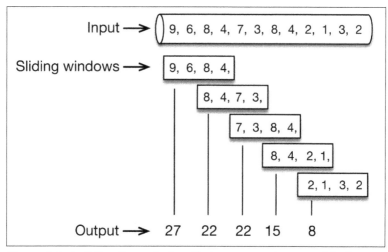

Figure 4-6. A sliding time window that computes the sum of the last minute's values every half minute.

In the first sliding window, the values 9, 6, 8, and 4 are summed up, yielding the result 27. Next, the window slides by a half minute (say, 2 values in our example), and the values 8, 4, 7, 3 are summed up, yielding the result 22, etc. A tumbling time window of 1 minute can be defined in Flink simply as:

```
stream.timeWindow(Time.minutes(1))
```

And a sliding time window of 1 minute that slides every 30 seconds can be defined as simply as:

```
stream.timeWindow(Time.minutes(1), Time.seconds(30))
```

Count Windows

Another common type of window supported by Flink is the *count* window. Here, we are grouping elements based on their counts instead of timestamps. For example, the sliding window in Figure 4-6 can also be interpreted as a count window of size 4 elements that slides every 2 elements. Tumbling and sliding count windows can be defined as simply as:

```
stream.countWindow(4)
stream.countWindow(4, 2)
```

Count windows, while useful, are less rigorously defined than time windows and should be used with care. Because time always goes on, a time window will always eventually "close." However, with a count window of, say, 100 elements, you might have a situation where there are never 100 elements for this key, which will lead to the window never closing, and the memory occupied by the window will remain garbage. One way to mitigate that is to couple a time window with a timeout using a trigger, which we will describe later in the section "Triggers".

Session Windows

Another very useful type of window provided by Flink is the *session* window. As mentioned briefly in Chapter 3, a session is a period of activity that is preceded and followed by a period of inactivity; for example, a series of interactions of a user on a website, followed by the user closing the browser tab or simply becoming inactive. Sessions need their own mechanism because they typically do not have a set duration (some sessions can be 30 seconds and another 1 hour), or a set number of interactions (some sessions can be 3 clicks followed by a purchase and another can be 40 clicks without a purchase).

Flink is currently the only open source stream processing engine that supports sessions.

Session windows in Flink are specified using a timeout. This basically specifies how long we want to wait until we believe that a session has ended. For example, here we expire a session when the user is inactive for five minutes:

```
stream.window(SessionWindows.withGap(Time.minutes(5)))
```

Triggers

In addition to windows, Flink also provides an optional mechanism to define *triggers*. Triggers control when the results are made available—in other words, when the contents of a window will be aggregated and returned to the user. Every default window comes coupled with a trigger. For example, a time window on event time is triggered when a watermark arrives. But as a user, you can also implement a custom trigger (for example, providing approximate early results of the window every 1 second) in addition to the complete and accurate results when the watermark arrives.

Implementation of Windows

Internally in Flink, all of these types of windows are implemented using the same mechanism. Although the internals of the mechanism are not important for basic users, it is important to note that:

- The windowing mechanism is completely separate from the checkpointing mechanism (discussed in detail in Chapter 5). This means that the window duration has no dependency on the checkpointing interval, and, indeed, one can define windows without a "duration" (e.g., the count and session windows we saw above).

- Advanced users can directly use the underlying mechanism to define more elaborate forms of windows (e.g., time windows that also produce an intermediate result based on count, or even a value of a specific record).

Time Travel

An aspect central to the streaming architecture is *time travel*. If all data processing is done by the stream processor, then how do we evolve applications, how do we process historical data, and how do we reprocess the data (say, for debugging or auditing purposes)? This idea is presented in Figure 4-7.

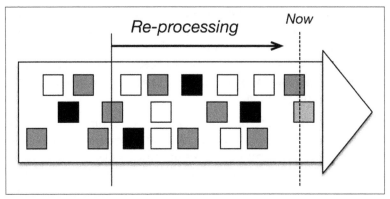

Figure 4-7. Time travel for data reprocessing. Support for event time by the stream processor means that rerunning the same program on the same data by rewinding the stream will yield the same results.

As shown in Figure 4-7, time travel means rewinding the stream to some time in the past and restarting the processing from there, eventually catching up with the present. Modern transport layers like Apache Kafka and MapR Streams support this functionality, setting them apart from older solutions. Whereas real-time stream processing always processes the last data (the "now") in the figure, historical stream processing starts from the past and (optionally) catches up with the present.

> To be able to travel back in time and reprocess the data correctly, the stream processor needs to support event time.

If windows are defined based on wall-clock time instead of the timestamps embedded in the records themselves, every time we run the same application, we will get a different result. Event time makes processing deterministic by guaranteeing that running the same application on the same stream will yield the same results.

Watermarks

We saw that support for event time is central to the streaming architecture, providing accuracy and the ability to reprocess data. When computation is based on event time, how do we know that all events have arrived, and that we can compute and output the result of a window? In other words, how do we keep track of event time and know that a certain event time has been reached in the input stream? To keep track of event time, we need some sort of clock that is driven by the data instead of the wall clocks of the machines performing the computation.

Consider the 1-minute tumbling windows of Figure 4-5. Assume that the first window starts at 10:00:00 (meaning 10 hours, 0 minutes, 0 seconds) and needs to sum up all values from 10:00:00 until 10:01:00. How do we know that the time is 10:01:00 when time is part of the records themselves? In other words, how do we know that an element with timestamp 10:00:59 will not arrive?

Flink achieves this via *watermarks*, a mechanism to advance event time. Watermarks are regular records embedded in the stream that, based on event time, inform computations that a certain time has been reached. When the aforementioned window receives a watermark with a time marker greater than 10:01:00 (for example, both a watermark with time marker 10:01:00 and a watermark with time marker 10:03:43 would work the same), it knows that no further records with a timestamp greater than the marker will occur; all events with time less than or equal to the timestamp have already occurred. It can then safely compute and emit the result of the window (the sum). With watermarks, event time progresses completely independently from processing time. For example, if a watermark is late ("late" being measured in processing time), this will not affect the correctness of the results, only the speed in which we get the results.

How Watermarks Are Generated

In Flink, the application developer generates watermarks, as doing so usually requires some knowledge of the domain. A perfect watermark is a watermark that can never be wrong; that is, no event will ever arrive after a watermark with an event time from before the watermark. Under special circumstances, the timestamp from the latest event might even be a perfect watermark. This could happen, for example, if our input is perfectly ordered. A heuristic watermark, in contrast, is just an estimate of the time progress, but can sometimes be wrong, meaning that some *late events* can come *after* the watermark that promised they would not come. Flink provides mechanisms to deal with late elements when watermarks are heuristic.

Domain knowledge is often used to specify a watermark. For example, we may know that our events might be late, but cannot possibly be more than five seconds late, which means that we can emit a watermark of the largest timestamp seen, minus five seconds. Or, a different Flink job may monitor the stream and construct a model for generating watermarks, learning from the lateness of the events as they arrive.

> Watermarks provide a (possibly heuristic) mechanism to specify the completeness of our input in event time.

If watermarks are too slow, we might see a slowdown in the speed with which we are getting output, but we can remedy that by emitting approximate results even before the watermark (Flink provides mechanisms for doing so). If watermarks are too fast, we might get a result that we think is correct but is not, and we can remedy that by using Flink's mechanisms for late data. If all of this seems complicated, remember that most event streams in the real world are out of order and that there is no such thing (usually) as perfect knowledge about how out of order they are. (In theory, we would have to look at the future for that.) Watermarks are the only mechanism that require us to deal with out-of-order data and to bound the correctness of our results; the alternative would be ignoring reality and pretending that our results are correct when they are not, without any bounds on their correctness.

A Real-World Example: Kappa Architecture at Ericsson

Motivated by the scale of data that a typical Ericsson-powered operator needs to process (10 to 100 terabytes per day, or 100,000 to 1,000,000 events per second), a team at Ericsson sought to implement a so-called "Kappa architecture."[2] This term was coined (somewhat tongue-in-cheek) by Jay Kreps, one of the creators of Apache Kafka in an O'Reilly Radar article in 2014 (*https://www.oreilly.com/ ideas/questioning-the-lambda-architecture*), as a critique to the so-called Lambda architecture. This is just another name for exactly the streaming architecture that we discussed in Chapter 2: the data stream is at the heart of the design; data sources are immutable; and a single-stream analytics framework, such as Apache Flink, is used to process both the fresh data as well as the historical data via stream replay.

The use case is real-time analysis of logs and system performance metrics of a live cloud infrastructure, to continuously monitor whether the cloud is behaving normally or showing a "novelty." A novelty can be either an anomalous behavior, or a change of the state in the system; for example, the addition of new virtual machines. The approach they took was to apply a Bayesian online learning model to a stream of various metrics (telemetry and log events) of a telco cloud monitoring system. In the words of Ericsson researchers Nicolas Seyvet and Ignacio Mulas Viela (*http://oreil.ly/ 2aKx9ZM*):

> The proposed method quickly detects anomalies with high accuracy while adapting (learning) over time to new system normals, making it a desirable tool for considerably reducing maintenance costs associated with operability of large computing infrastructures.

The data pipeline that the Ericsson team built is shown in Figure 4-8.

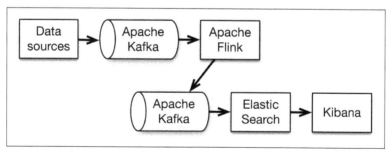

Figure 4-8. Streaming architecture using Apache Flink at Ericsson.

---

2 This section is based on the work by Nicolas Seyvet and Ignacio Mulas Viela, presented at Flink Forward 2015 (*http://bit.ly/2aSHNkX*) and at Strata/Hadoop World London 2016 (*http://oreil.ly/2aKx9ZM*).

The raw data pushed to Kafka is telemetry and log events from all physical and virtual machines in the cloud. Then, different Flink jobs consume this data and write them back to Kafka topics, from which they are pushed to Elastic Search and Kibana, a search index and visualization system, respectively. This architecture allows each Flink job to perform a well-defined task, as the output of one job can be used as input of another. For example, the pipeline to detect anomalies in the equipment is shown in Figure 4-9, where every intermediate stream is a Kafka topic (named for the data assigned to it), and every rectangle is a Flink job.

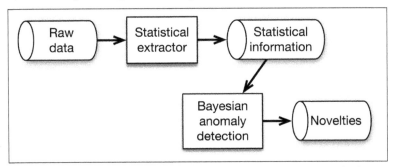

Figure 4-9. The data processing pipeline at Ericsson for anomaly detection uses Flink for the statistical extractor application and for anomaly detection.

So, why is Flink's support for event time important for this application? There are two reasons:

1. *Correctly classifying anomalies:* Timing is crucial for deciding upon an anomaly. For example, lots of logging events being generated at the same time is often a predictor of something being wrong. In order to group and classify those events correctly, it is important to take into account the time at which these events were actually generated (rather than the time we see them in the processing pipeline).

2. *Using stream-first architecture:* In the streaming architecture, the stream processor is used for all computations. The way to evolve applications is to repeat their execution in the stream processor; running the same data twice through a computation must produce the same result, and this is only possible when operating on event time.

CHAPTER 5

Stateful Computation

Streaming computation can be either *stateless* or *stateful*. A stateless program looks at each individual event and creates some output based on that last event. For example, a streaming program might receive temperature readings from a sensor and raise an alert if the temperature goes beyond 90 degrees. A stateful program creates output based on multiple events taken together. Examples of stateful programs include:

- All types of windows that we discussed in Chapter 4. For example, getting the average temperature reported by a sensor over the last hour is a stateful computation.

- All kinds of state machines used for complex event processing (CEP). For example, creating an alert after receiving 2 temperature readings that differ by more than 20 degrees within 1 minute is a stateful computation.

- All kinds of joins between streams as well as joins between streams, and static or slowly changing tables.

Figure 5-1 exemplifies the main difference between stateless and stateful stream processing. A stateless program (a transformation of black records to white records in the figure) receives each record separately (black input) and produces each output record based on the last input record alone (white records). A stateful program maintains state that is updated based on every input and produces output (gray records) based on the last input and the current value of the state.

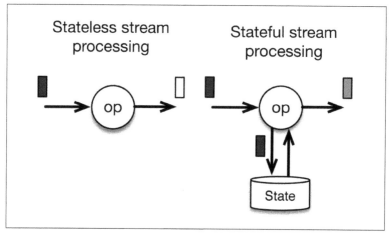

Figure 5-1. Stateless and stateful processing are compared here. Input records are shown as black bars. The left diagram shows how a stateless operation transforms each input record at a time and outputs each result based solely on that last record or event (white bar). The diagram on the right shows that a stateful program maintains the value of state for all of the records processed so far and updates it with each new input, such that the output (gray bar) reflects results that take into account more than one event.

While stateless computation is important by itself, the most interesting applications of stream processing as was just described are stateful. It also turns out that stateful computation is a lot more challenging to implement correctly than stateless computation. Whereas older stream processing systems did not provide support for stateful computations, the newer group of stream processors are all about state and guaranteeing the existence and correctness of that state under various failure scenarios.

Notions of Consistency

When we include state in a distributed system, naturally the question of consistency is raised. Consistency is, really, a different word for "level of correctness"; that is, how correct are my results after a failure and a successful recovery compared to what I would have gotten without any failures? For example, assume that we are simply counting user logins within the last hour. What is the count (the state) if the system experiences a failure? In the terminology of the stream processing world, people distinguish between three different levels of consistency:

- *At most once*: At most once is really a euphemism for no correctness guarantees whatsoever—the count may be lost after a failure.

- *At least once*: At least once, in our setting, means that the counter value may be bigger than but never smaller than the correct count. So, our program may over-count (in a failure scenario) but guarantees that it will never under-count.

- *Exactly once*: Exactly once means that the system guarantees that the count will be exactly the same as it would be in the failure-free scenario.

It used to be that at least once was very popular in the industry, with the first stream processors (Apache Storm, Apache Samza) guaranteeing only at least once when they first came out. This was the case for two reasons:

1. It is trickier to implement systems that guarantee exactly once. Exactly once is challenging at both the fundamental level (to decide what correct means exactly, and what is the scope of exactly once), and at the implementation level.

2. Early adopters of stream processing were willing to work around the framework limitations at the application level (e.g., by making their applications idempotent or simply redoing all calculations using a batch compute layer).

The first solutions that provided exactly once (Trident, Spark Streaming) came at a substantial cost in terms of performance and expressiveness. In order to guarantee exactly once behavior, these systems do not apply the application logic to each record separately, but instead process several (a batch of) records at a time, guaranteeing that either the processing of each batch will succeed as a whole or not at all. This situation implies that you have to wait for a batch to complete before getting any results. For this reason, users were often left having to use two stream processing frameworks together (one for exactly once and one for per-element, low-latency processing), resulting in even more complexity in the infrastructure. Guaranteeing exactly once and having low latency and efficiency used to be a tradeoff that users had to navigate. In contrast, Apache Flink does away with that tradeoff.

 One significant value that Flink has brought to the industry is that it is able to provide exactly once guarantees, low-latency processing, and high throughput all at once.

Essentially, Flink eliminates these tradeoffs by allowing a single framework to handle all requirements, a meaningful technological leap in the industry, which, like all such leaps, seems magical from the outside but makes a lot of sense when explained.

Flink Checkpoints: Guaranteeing Exactly Once

How does Flink guarantee exactly once processing? Flink makes use of a feature known as "checkpoints" as a way to reset to the correct state in the case of a failure. Consider this simple analogy to understand the role of checkpoints.

Suppose that you and a couple of friends are manually counting beads strung on circular necklaces, as depicted in Figure 5-2. You start at the clasp and slide the beads across through your fingers as you count, adding to the sum each time you slide a bead. Your friends are doing the same thing, each on their own string of beads. But what happens when you are momentarily distracted and lose count? If there are a lot of beads, you don't want to have to go back and start over, particularly if all three of you count at different speeds and are trying to coordinate your counts, for example, or if you want to write down how many beads all of you have counted during the last minute. (Remember tumbling time windows from Chapter 4.)

Figure 5-2. Counting beads in a circular string may seem a futile task, (even a bit Sisyphean because the counting never stops) but it serves as a good analogy to processing a never-ending stream of events, and is still a favorite activity to pass the time in some cultures ("worry beads").

So you devise a better system: you loosely tie colored ribbons at various intervals along each necklace, between the beads, such that these ribbon markers can be slid along with the beads. You get a helper to act as a central authority to keep track of the sums that you and your friends call out each time you reach a ribbon marker. That way, if someone messes up and needs to restart, it doesn't cause everyone to have to go all the way back to the clasp and start over. Instead, you alert the others to the problem and all of you go back to the last colored ribbon marker, and then the helper (central authority) tells each of you your count "as of the pink ribbon," for instance, and you start incrementing your count from that sum.

Flink checkpoints behave in a manner analogous to the ribbon markers. The key idea in this analogy is that each bead clearly sits either before or after a particular ribbon along the string; that makes the ribbon a reference point for a reset of the count (current state) if needed. The overall state (sum of beads) is updated with each bead that is counted, and the central authority saves the checkpoint state related to each ribbon. In other words, how many beads were counted when you hit the pink ribbon? The orange ribbon? That makes it easy to restart the count if a problem occurs.

 Checkpoints are one of the most valuable innovations in Flink because they are the key to providing exactly once guarantees without trading off performance.

Essentially, the role of Flink checkpoints is to guarantee correct state, even after a program interruption. With this basic concept in mind, let's look under the covers at an example of how Flink checkpoints operate. Flink offers the user facilities to define state. For example, the following Scala program maintains the count of the second field of the input, grouping by the first field of the input (a string):

```scala
val stream: DataStream[(String, Int)] = ...

val counts: DataStream[(String, Int)] = stream
  .keyBy(record => record._1)
  .mapWithState((in: (String, Int), count: Option[Int]) =>
    count match {
      case Some(c) => ( (in._1, c + in._2), Some(c + in._2) )
      case None => ( (in._1, in._2), Some(in._2) )
    })
```

There are two operators in the program: the keyBy operator groups the incoming records by the first element (a string), repartitions the data based on that key, and forwards the records to the next operator: the stateful map operator. The map operator receives each element, advances the count by adding up the second field of the input record to the current count, and emits the element with the updated now count. Figure 5-3 shows the starting condition with all of the six records in the input stream intercepted by checkpoint barriers and the state of all map operators being zero (nothing counted yet). All the records with key "a" will be processed by the top map operator, all records with key "b" will be processed by the middle map operator, and all records with key "c" will be processed by the bottom map operator.

Consider the program above and think about how checkpoints can provide guarantees as you process six records in the input with execution that is spread across three parallel instances (nodes, cores, etc.).

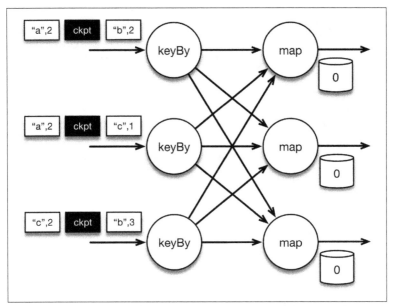

Figure 5-3. Starting condition for the program. Note that initial state for record groups a, b, and c is zero in each case, shown as values on the three cylinders. Checkpoint barriers are shown as black "ckpt" records. Each record is strictly before or after a checkpoint in sequence of processing; e.g., ("b",2) is to be processed before the top checkpoint and ("a",2) after it.

Checkpoint barriers are just like regular records. They are processed by the operators, but instead of contributing to the result of the computation (as do the records that carry data), checkpoint barriers trigger actions related to *checkpointing*. When a data source that is reading from the input stream (inlined with the keyBy operator in our example) sees a checkpoint barrier, it saves the position of this record. This would be the offset, when the input stream is served from the message transport (either Apache Kafka or MapR Streams), to a stable storage mechanism. The storage mechanism can be pluggable in Flink and might be a distributed file system like HDFS, S3, or MapR-FS, for example. This situation is depicted in Figure 5-4.

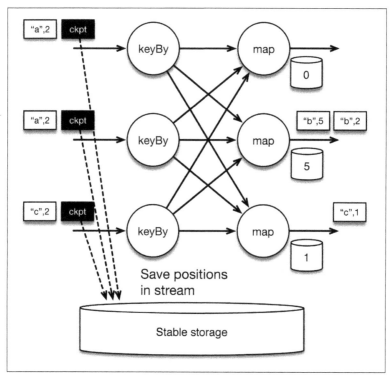

Figure 5-4. When a Flink data source (here inlined with the keyBy operator) encounters a checkpoint barrier, it records the position of the barrier in the input stream to stable storage. This step will allow Flink to later restart the input from that position.

Checkpoint barriers flow through the edges between operators like regular records. When the map operators receive the checkpoint barriers after they have processed the first three records, they will write out their state asynchronously to stable storage. This action is depicted in Figure 5-5.

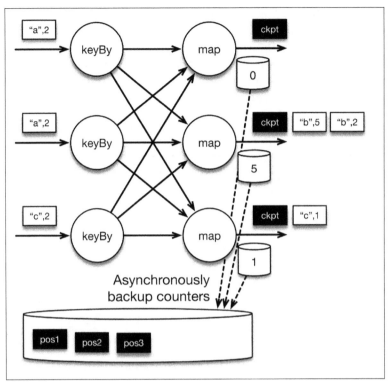

Figure 5-5. Condition of the program after all records prior to the checkpoint (records ["b",2], [b,"3"], and ["c",1]) have been processed by the stateful map operators. At this point, the positions of the checkpoint barriers in the input stream have already been backed up in stable storage—this backup occurred when the checkpoint barriers were processed by the source operators. The map operators are now processing the checkpoint barriers, triggering an asynchronous backup of their state in stable storage.

Once the backup of the states of the map operators and the positions of the barriers in the input streams has been acknowledged, the checkpoint can be marked as successful, as depicted in Figure 5-6. What we achieved was to take a snapshot of the state of the computation at a logical time (the time denoted by the positions of the barriers in the input streams), without ever stopping or blocking the computation. By making sure that the backed-up states and positions refer to the same logical time, we will later see how—by restoring the computation from that backup—we can achieve exactly once state guarantees. Note that when there is no failure, the overhead of

Flink checkpointing is minimal, and the speed of checkpointing is driven by the available bandwidth to stable storage. Recall the string of beads example: the ribbons just pass by unless someone loses count and needs to use them. (There is work underway in Flink to save only changes to the state rather than the value of the state, which makes this overhead even smaller.)

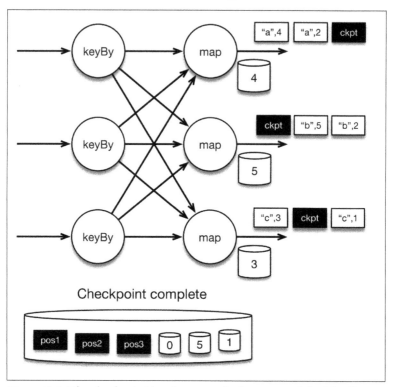

Figure 5-6. The checkpoint has been marked as successful with all states, and input stream positions have been backed up to stable storage. All records in the input have been processed. Note that the state values in backup and the actual state values are different. Those in the backup reflect the state as of the checkpoint.

If writing the checkpoint fails for some reason, Flink will discard that checkpoint and continue execution as normal because one of the later checkpoints may succeed. The guarantees for the state remain just as strong, although recovery may take a bit longer. Only if a number of consecutive checkpoints fail will Flink register an error, as this is usually an indication of something going seriously and persistently wrong.

Consider now the situation in Figure 5-7, with the checkpoint having successfully completed and a failure occurring right *after* the checkpoint.

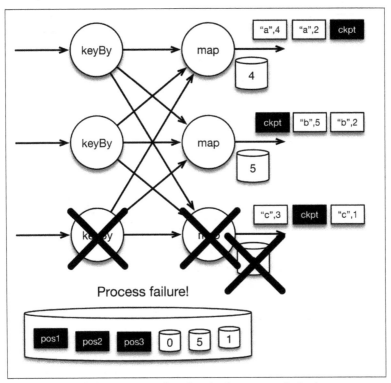

Figure 5-7. A failure occurs after the checkpoint, with the bottommost instance being lost.

Flink will then restart the topology (possibly acquiring new execution resources), rewind the input stream to the positions registered in the last checkpoint, and restore the state values and continue execution from there. In our example, this means that records ("a",2), ("a",2), and ("c",2) will be replayed.

This reprocessing is depicted in Figure 5-8. Starting the computation again from that point will guarantee that the value of the map operator states will be as if no failure had ever occurred after the remaining records have been processed. Note, however, that the output stream will contain duplicates. In particular, the records (`"a"`, 2), (`"a"`,4) and (`"c"`,3) will appear twice. This problem can be avoided when Flink writes the output stream to specific output systems (e.g., file systems or databases), as discussed later in this chapter.

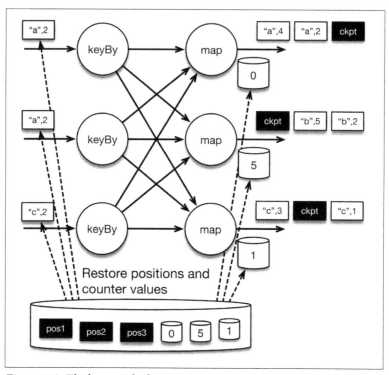

Figure 5-8. Flink rewinds the input stream to the positions of the last barriers, as recorded in the checkpoint, and restores the states of the map operators to the ones that had been recorded in the last checkpoint. Flink then simply restarts the processing from here. This guarantees that after the records have been processed, the state of the map operators will be as if no failure had ever occurred.

The algorithm used for checkpointing in Flink is formally called *Asynchronous Barrier Snapshotting* (*https://arxiv.org/abs/1506.08603*). The algorithm is loosely based on the seminal Chandy-Lamport algorithm for distributed snapshots.

Savepoints: Versioning State

Previously, we saw that checkpoints are automatically generated by Flink to provide a way to reprocess records while correcting state in case of a failure. But Flink users also have a way to consciously manage versions of state through a feature called *savepoints*.

A savepoint is taken in exactly the same way as a checkpoint but is triggered manually by the user (using the Flink command-line tools or the web console) instead of by Flink itself. Like checkpoints, savepoints are also stored in stable storage and give the user the ability to start a new version of the job or to restart the job from a savepoint rather than from a beginning in time. You can think of savepoints as snapshots of a job at a certain time (the time that the savepoint was taken).

Another way to think about savepoints is saving versions of the application state at well-defined times. This is similar to saving versions of applications themselves using version control systems. The simplest example is taking snapshots at regular intervals without changing the code of the application—that is, keeping the application version *as is*. This situation is depicted in Figure 5-9.

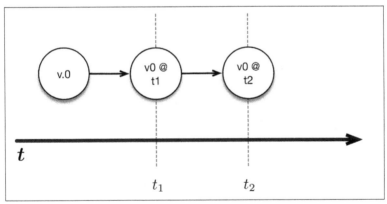

Figure 5-9. Savepoints (represented by circles) are triggered manually to capture the state of a running Flink application at different times.AU

Here, we have a running version of an application (version 0) and took a savepoint of our application at time t1 and a savepoint at t2. At any given time, we could go back and restart the program from these times. Even more significant, we are able to start a modified version of a program from a savepoint. For example, we can change the code of the application (let's call it version 0.1) and start it from the savepoint taken at t1. In this way, we have both version 0 and version 0.1 of the programs running at the same time while taking subsequent savepoints to both versions at later times, as shown in Figure 5-10.

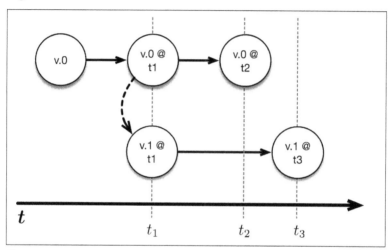

Figure 5-10. Using savepoints to advance the version of a Flink application. The new version can be started from a savepoint created by an older version.

You can use savepoints to solve a variety of production issues for streaming jobs:

1. *Application code upgrades*: Assume that you have found a bug in an already running application and you want the future events to be processed by the updated code with the bug fixed. By taking a savepoint of the job and restarting from that savepoint using the new code, downstream applications will not see the difference (except for the update of course).

2. *Flink version upgrades*: Upgrading Flink itself also becomes easy because you can take savepoints of running pipelines and replay them from the savepoints using an upgraded Flink version.

3. *Maintenance and migration*: Using savepoints, you can easily "pause and resume" an application. This is especially useful for cluster maintenance as well as migrating jobs consistently to a new cluster. In addition, this is useful for developing, testing,

and debugging applications, as you do not need to replay the complete event stream.

4. *What-if simulations (reinstatements)*: Many times, it is very useful to run an alternative application logic to model "what-if" scenarios from controllable points in the past.

5. *A/B testing*: By running two different versions of application code in parallel from the exact same savepoint, you can model A/B testing scenarios.

All of these issues occur in the real world. Flink's internal checkpointing mechanism surfaces as savepoints, solving issues like the ones described here. This reflects that concept that Flink's checkpoint feature is essentially a programmable mechanism to consistently upgrade state versions, much like a database system with multiversion concurrency control. This fundamental characteristic of the checkpoint mechanism will surface again when we look at how to provide end-to-end consistency in the next section.

End-to-End Consistency and the Stream Processor as a Database

We have seen how Flink can guarantee that state is kept consistent (exactly once) in a simple application that counts or aggregates data. Let us now look at this application end-to-end, as it might be deployed in production (depicted in Figure 5-11).

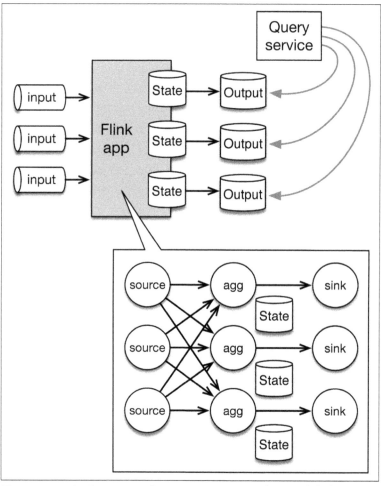

Figure 5-11. Application architecture consisting of a stateful Flink application consuming data from a message queue and writing data to an output system used for querying. The callout shows what goes on inside the Flink application.

A partitioned storage system (e.g., a message queue such as Kafka or MapR Streams) serves as the data input. The Flink topology, shown as a callout in Figure 5-11, consists of three operators: the data source reads data from the input, partitions it by key, and routes records to instances of the stateful operators, which can be a `map WithState` as we saw in the previous section, a window aggregation, etc. This operator writes the contents of the state (the counts in our previous example) or some derivative results to a sink, which transfers these to a partitioned storage system (e.g., a file system or a database) that serves as output storage. A query service (e.g., the database's query API) then allows users to query the state (in the simplest case, the counts) as they were written in the output storage. Note that the figure depicts the contents of the state written to the output.

Keep in mind that, in this case, the output reflects the contents of the state in the Flink application as of the time it was last written out.

The first question is, how can we transfer the contents of the state to the output with exactly once guarantees? (This is called end-to-end exactly once.) There are essentially two ways to do that, and the right way depends on the nature of the system used for output and the application requirements:

1. The first way is to buffer all output at the sink and commit this atomically when the sink receives a checkpoint record. This method ensures that the output storage system only contains results that are guaranteed to be consistent and that duplicates will never be visible. Essentially, the output storage takes part in Flink's checkpointing. For this to work, the output storage system needs to provide the ability to atomically commit.

2. The second way is to eagerly write data to the output, keeping in mind that some of this data might be "dirty" and replayed after a failure. If there is a failure, then we need to roll back the output, in addition to the input and the Flink job, thus overwriting the dirty data and effectively deleting dirty data that has already been written to the output. Note that even with this way, in many cases there will be no deletions. For example, if new records are only overwriting old records (and not adding to the output), then the dirty values will be transient only between checkpoints and eventually overridden by new and refined values.

Note that these two alternatives correspond exactly to two well-known levels of isolation in relational database systems: *read committed* and *read uncommitted*. Read committed guarantees that all reads (queries to the output) will read committed data and no intermediate, in-flight, or dirty data. Subsequent reads may return different results because the data may have changed. Read uncommitted does allow dirty reads; in other words, the queries always see the latest version of data as it is being processed.

For some applications, weaker semantics may be acceptable, so Flink provides several build-in sinks with multiple semantics; for example, a distributed filesink with read uncommitted semantics (for a full list, visit the current Flink documentation (*http://bit.ly/2biNERs*)). Depending on the capabilities of the output system and the application requirements, the user can choose the right semantics.

We saw that, depending on the type of output, Flink together with the corresponding connector can provide exactly once guarantees end-to- end with a variety of isolation levels.

Now, recall the application architecture shown in Figure 5-11. One reason for the output storage system here is that the state inside Flink is not accessible to the outside world in this example, so the output storage is the target of the query. If, however, we would be able to query the state in the stateful operator (the counts in this case), we might not even need to have an output system in certain situations where the state contains all the information needed for the query. This is true for a variety of applications, and in these cases, *querying the state directly* can lead to the vastly simplified architecture shown in Figure 5-12 as well as to vastly improved performance.

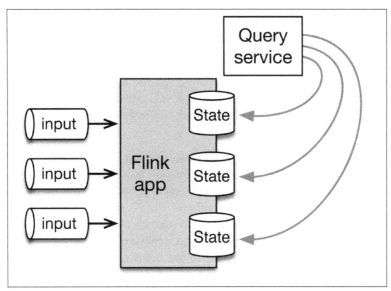

Figure 5-12. Simplified application architecture using Flink's queryable state. For those cases when the state is all the information that is needed, querying the state directly can improve performance.

Queryable state is currently a work in progress by the Flink community. With queryable state, Flink offers a query API to issue read requests to Flink and get the current value of the state. In some sense, in a limited number of scenarios, Flink becomes a replacement for a database system, offering both a write path (the input stream that changes the state) as well as a read path (queryable state). Although this makes sense for a lot of applications, queryable state is definitely more limited than a general-purpose database.

Flink Performance: the Yahoo! Streaming Benchmark

Apache Flink performance was tested in several different ways through a sequence of variations using the Yahoo! Streaming Benchmark.

Original Application with the Yahoo! Streaming Benchmark

In December 2015, the Storm team at Yahoo! published a blog post (*http://bit.ly/2bhgMJd*) benchmarking Apache Storm, Apache Flink, and Apache Spark. This was a very valuable contribution to the industry, as it was the first benchmark in the field that was based on a real-world application.

The application consumes ad impressions from Apache Kafka, looks up which ad campaign the ad corresponds to (from Redis), and computes the number of ad views in each 10-second window, grouped by campaign. The final results of the 10-second windows are written to Redis for storage, and the statuses of those windows are also written to Redis every second in order for users to be able to query them in real time. In the initial benchmark, because Storm was a stateless stream processor (i.e., it did not provide facilities to define and maintain state), the Flink job was also written in a stateless fashion, with all state being stored in Redis, as depicted in Figure 5-13.

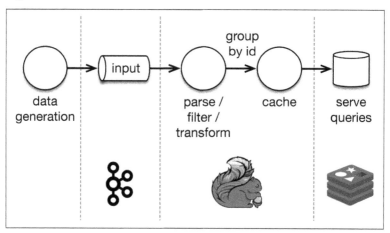

Figure 5-13. The job used in the Yahoo! streaming benchmark. The data processors being tested were Spark Streaming, Storm, and Flink (although we've included only the Flink logo in our graphic of the data architecture).

The results of that experiment are summarized in the simplified graph in Figure 5-14.

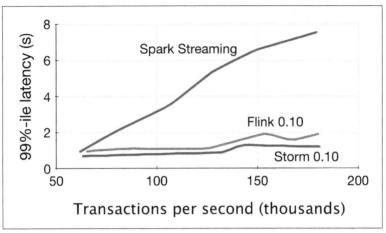

Figure 5-14. Results from the original Yahoo! streaming benchmark. The x-axis is throughput in thousands of events per second, and the y-axis is the 99th percentile end-to-end latency (meaning that 99% of events arrive within this latency) in seconds for the given throughput. See the Yahoo! team's blog post (http://bit.ly/2bhgMJd) for a more detailed graph and additional results.

As Figure 5-14 shows, in this benchmark, Spark Streaming suffered from a throughput-latency tradeoff. As batches increase in size, latency also increases. If batches are kept small to improve latency, throughput decreases. Storm and Flink can both sustain low latency as throughput increases.

In order to further test Flink performance in terms of velocity, a number of different conditions were set up and tested step by step.

First Modification: Using Flink State

The original benchmark focused on measuring end-to-end latency at relatively low throughput, even at the maximum, and did not focus on implementing these applications in a fault-tolerant manner. Additionally, the application had a very small key cardinality (in the 100s), which does not extend to applications with many users, or to a key space that grows over time (e.g., tweets). An extension of this benchmark, published on February 2, 2016 at the data Artisans blog (*http://data-artisans.com/extending-the-yahoo-streaming-benchmark/*), focused on addressing these points. With Spark out of the game as an unacceptable solution by the original benchmark, the extension focused on Storm and Flink, which showed seemingly similar behavior in the original benchmark.

The first change was to reimplement the Flink application to use the facilities that are provided by Flink for state fault tolerance, as shown in Figure 5-15. These changes made the application exactly once.

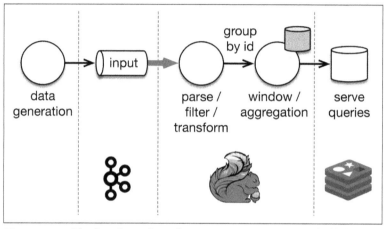

Figure 5-15. The benchmark application rewritten to use Flink's built-in state. With this change, the application can sustain a throughput of 3 million events per second and has exactly once guarantees. The application is now bottlenecked on the connection between the Flink cluster and the Kafka cluster (red arrow).

Second Modification: Increase Volume Through Improved Data Generator

The second step in extending the benchmark to test velocity was to scale up the volume of the input stream by writing a data generator that can produce millions of events per second. The results for this modification are shown in Figure 5-16.

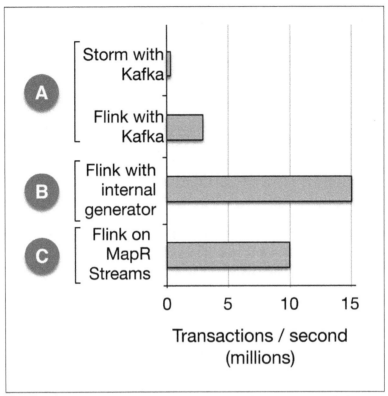

*Figure 5-16. Results using the higher-volume data generator: (A)
When using Storm with Kafka, the benchmark application can sustain
400,000 events per second and is CPU-bound, whereas in the case of
Flink with Kafka, the application can sustain 3 million events per second and is network-bound. (B) By removing the streaming component
to avoid the network bottleneck, the Flink application can sustain 15
million events per second. (C) An additional test was done with the
streaming transport component provided by MapR Streams and 10
high-performance nodes (different hardware from A and B); the Flink
application can sustain 10 million events per second.*

Storm could keep up with the load until about 400,000 events per
second, at which point the system became CPU-bound. Flink could
keep up until 3 million events per second (a 7.5x difference), at
which point the system became network-bound between the Kafka
cluster and the Flink cluster.

Third Modification: Dealing with Network Bottleneck

In order to see what Flink performance could be without the issue of the network bottleneck. the data generator was moved into the Flink job. This workflow is illustrated in the diagram in Figure 5-17. Under these conditions, Flink was able to sustain a volume of 15 million events per second (a 37.5x difference) as shown in Figure 5-16 (B). Having the data generator integrated into the Flink application allows the limits of performance to be tested, but this is not an entirely realistic configuration since real-world data would have to be streamed into an application from outside the application.

We note that this is definitely not a Kafka limitation—Kafka can sustain such throughput and more—but merely a limitation of the hardware setup used for these experiments, where the network connection between the Kafka cluster and Flink cluster was slow.

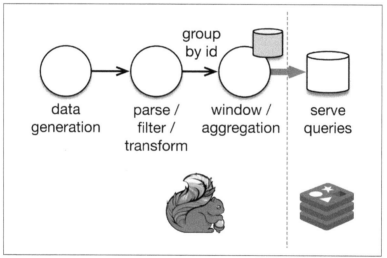

Figure 5-17. Eliminating the network bottleneck by making the data generator part of the Flink program makes the system able to sustain a throughput of 15 million events per second. After increasing the key cardinality, the bottleneck becomes the writes to Redis every 1 second. This is not a production configuration, but it is intended to test the limits of what Flink can do.

Fourth Modification: Using MapR Streams

A different way to avoid a network bottleneck and test Flink performance at scale was to run the benchmark by using MapR Streams
for streaming transport. In a separate benchmark, the same application was run with a separate data generator, but configured to send
the generated data through MapR Streams to the Flink application.

With MapR, streaming is integrated into the platform, which allows
Flink to run colocated with the data generator tasks and with all data
transport and thus avoiding most of the issue of network connectivity between a Kafka cluster and a Flink cluster. In this high-
performance configuration and on hardware with faster networking,
Flink was able to sustain a processing rate of 10 million events per
second. These results are shown in Figure 5-16(C).

Fifth Modification: Increased Cardinality and Direct Query

The final extension of the benchmark was to increase the key cardinality (number of ad campaigns). The original benchmark had
only 100 distinct keys, which were flushed every second to Redis so
that they could be made queryable. When the key cardinality is
increased to 1 million, the overall system throughput reduces to
280,000 events per second, as the bottleneck of the system becomes
the transfer of this data to Redis. Using an early prototype of Flink's
queryable state (as in Figure 5-18), this bottleneck disappears, and
the system can again sustain 15 million events per second, with millions of keys being available for querying, as depicted in Figure 5-19.

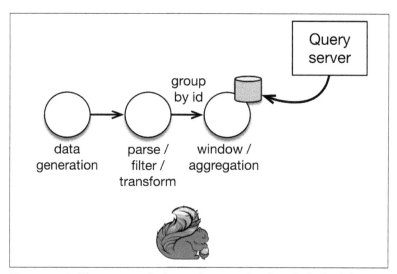

Figure 5-18. Eliminating the key-value store bottleneck for high key cardinalities.

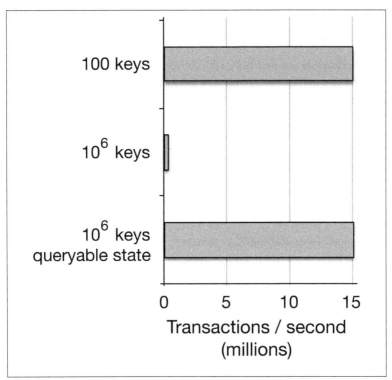

Figure 5-19. By moving the querying inside a prototype of Flink's queryable state, the system can sustain a throughput of 15 million events per second even when key cardinality is very high.

So, what does this use case teach us? By avoiding streaming bottlenecks and by using Flink's stateful stream processing abilities, we were able to get almost a 30x increase in throughput compared to Storm while still guaranteeing exactly once processing with high availability. Roughly speaking, this means that we can pay for 30 times less hardware or cloud credits, or that we can handle problems that are 30 times the size, with the same hardware.

Conclusion

In this chapter, we saw how stateful stream processing changes the rules of the game. By having checkpointed state as a first-class citizen inside the stream processor, we can get correct results after failures, very high throughput, and low latency all at the same time, completely eliminating past tradeoffs that people thought of as fundamental (but are not). This is one of the most important advantages of Flink.

Another advantage of Flink is its ability to handle streaming and batch using a single technology, completely eliminating the need for a dedicated batch layer. Chapter 6 provides a brief overview of how batch processing with Flink is possible.

Batch Is a Special Case of Streaming

So far in this book, we have been talking about unbounded stream processing—that is, processing data from some time continuously and forever. This condition is depicted in Figure 6-1.

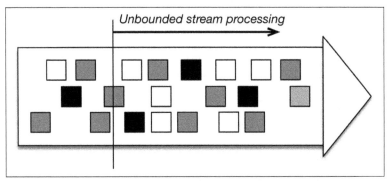

Figure 6-1. Unbounded stream processing: the input does not have an end, and data processing starts from the present or some point in the past and continues indefinitely.

A different style of processing is *bounded stream processing*, or processing data from some starting time until some end time, as depicted in Figure 6-2. The input data might be naturally bounded (meaning that it is a data set that does not grow over time), or it can be artificially bounded for analysis purposes (meaning that we are only interested in events within some time bounds).

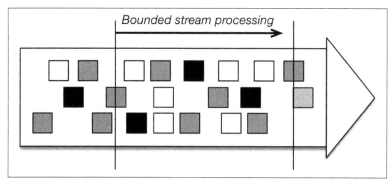

Figure 6-2. Bounded stream processing: the input has a beginning and an end, and data processing stops after some time.

Bounded stream processing is clearly a special case of unbounded stream processing; data processing just happens to stop at some point. In addition, when the results of the computation are not produced continuously during execution, but only once at the end, we have the case called *batch processing* (data is processed "as a batch").

Batch processing is a very special case of stream processing; instead of defining a sliding or tumbling window over the data and producing results every time the window slides, we define a global window, with all records belonging to the same window. For example, a simple Flink program that counts visitors in a website every hour, grouped by region continuously, is the following:

```
val counts = visits
  .keyBy("region")
  .timeWindow(Time.hours(1))
  .sum("visits")
```

If we know that our input data set was already bounded, we can get the equivalent "batch" program by writing:

```
val counts = visits
  .keyBy("region")
  .window(GlobalWindows.create)
  .trigger(EndOfTimeTrigger.create)
  .sum("visits")
```

Flink is unusual in that it can process data as a continuous stream or as bounded streams (batch). With Flink, you process bounded data streams also by using Flink's DataSet API, which is made for exactly that purpose. The above program in Flink's DataSet API would look like this:

```
val counts = visits
  .groupBy("region")
  .sum("visits")
```

This program will produce the same results when we know that the input is bounded, but it looks friendlier to a programmer accustomed to using batch processors.

Batch Processing Technology

In principle, batch processing is a special case of stream processing: when the input is bounded and we want only the final result at the end, it suffices to define a global window over the complete data set and perform the computation on that window. But how efficient is it?

Traditionally, dedicated batch processors are used to process bounded data streams, and there are cases where this approach is more efficient than using the stream processor naively as described above. However, it is possible to integrate most optimizations necessary for efficient large-scale batch processing in a stream processor. This approach is what Flink does, and it works very efficiently (as shown in Figure 6-3).

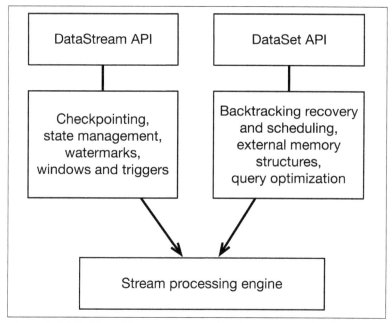

Figure 6-3. Flink's architecture supports both stream and batch processing styles, with one underlying engine.

The same backend (the stream processing engine) is used for both bounded and unbounded data processing. On top of the stream processing engine, Flink overlays the following mechanisms:

- A *checkpointing* mechanism and *state* mechanism to ensure fault-tolerant, stateful processing
- The *watermark* mechanism to ensure event-time clock
- Available *windows* and *triggers* to bound the computation and define when to make results available

A different code path in Flink overlays different mechanisms on top of the same stream processing engine to ensure efficient batch processing. Although reviewing these in detail are beyond the scope of this book, the most important mechanisms are:

- Backtracking for scheduling and recovery: the mechanism introduced by Microsoft Dryad and now used by almost every batch processor

- Special memory data structures for hashing and sorting that can partially spill data from memory to disk when needed
- An optimizer that tries to transform the user program to an equivalent one that minimizes the time to result

At the time of writing, these two code paths result in two different APIs (the DataStream API and the DataSet API), and one cannot create a Flink job that mixes the two and takes advantage of all of Flink's capabilities. However, this need not be the case; in fact, the Flink community is discussing a unified API that includes the capabilities of both APIs. And the Apache Beam (incubating) community has created exactly that: an API for both batch and stream processing that generates Flink programs for execution.

Case Study: Flink as a Batch Processor

At the Flink Forward 2015 conference, Dongwon Kim (then a post-doctoral researcher at POSTECH in South Korea) presented a benchmarking study that he conducted comparing MapReduce, Tez, Spark, and Flink at pure batch processing tasks: TeraSort and a distributed hash join.[1]

The first task, TeraSort, comes from the annual terabyte sort competition, which measures the elapsed time to sort 1 terabyte of data. In the context of these systems, TeraSort is essentially a distributed sort problem, consisting of the following phases, depicted in Figure 6-4:

1. A read phase reads the data partitions from files on HDFS
2. A local sort partially sorts these partitions
3. A shuffle phase redistributes the data by key to the processing nodes
4. A final sort phase produces the sorted output
5. A write phase writes out the sorted partitions to files on HDFS

---

1 See the slides and video of the talk at *http://2015.flink-forward.org/?session=a-comparative-performance-evaluation-of-flink*. (*http://2015.flink-forward.org/?session=a-comparative-performance-evaluation-of-flink*)

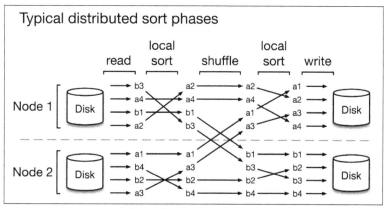

Figure 6-4. Processing phases for distributed sort.

A TeraSort implementation is included with the Apache Hadoop distribution, and you can use the same implementation unchanged with Apache Tez, given that Tez can execute programs written in the MapReduce API. The Spark and Flink implementations were provided by the author of that presentation and are available at *https://github.com/eastcirclek/terasort*. The cluster that was used for the measurements consisted of 42 machines with 12 cores, 24 GB of memory, and 6 hard disk drives each.

The results of the benchmark, depicted in Figure 6-5, show that Flink performs the sorting task in less time than all other systems. MapReduce took 2,157 seconds, Tez took 1,887 seconds, Spark took 2,171 seconds, and Flink took 1,480 seconds.

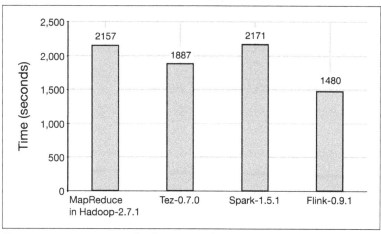

Figure 6-5. TeraSort results for MapReduce, Tez, Spark, and Flink.

The second task was a distributed join between a large (240 GB) and a small (256 MB) data set. There, Flink was also the fastest system, outperforming Tez by 2x and Spark by 4x. These results are shown in Figure 6-6.

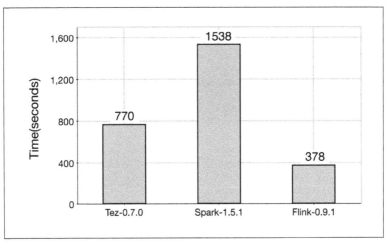

Figure 6-6. HashJoin results for Tez, Spark, and Flink.

The overall reason for these results is that Flink execution is stream-based, which means that the processing stages that we described above overlap more, and shuffling is pipelined, which leads to much fewer disk accesses. In contrast, execution with MapReduce, Tez, and Spark is batch-based, which means that data is written to disk before it's sent over the network. In the end, this means less idle time and fewer disk accesses when using Flink.

We note that as with all benchmarks, the raw numbers might be quite different in different cluster setups, configurations, and software versions. While the numbers themselves might be different now compared to when that benchmark was conducted (indeed, the software versions used for that benchmark were Hadoop 2.7.1, Tez 0.7.0, Spark 1.5.1, and Flink 0.9.1, which have all been superseded with newer releases), the main point is that with the right optimizations, a stream processor (Flink) can perform equally as well as, or better than, even batch processors (MapReduce, Tez, Spark) in tasks that are on the home turf of batch processors. Consequently, with Flink, it is possible to cover processing of both unbounded data streams and bounded data streams with one data processing framework without sacrificing performance.

Additional Resources

Going Further with Apache Flink

By now, we hope that we have whet your appetite and you are ready to get started with Apache Flink. What's the best way to do that? The Flink open source project website is *https://flink.apache.org/*. This website maintains a "quickstart (*https://ci.apache.org/projects/flink/flink-docs-master/quickstart/run_example_quickstart.html*)" guide. In just a few minutes, you will be able to write your first stream processing program. The site even includes an example that allows you to ingest and analyze all edits being made around the world to Wikipedia.org.

If you prefer something more visual, a post on the MapR blog shows you how to use Flink to ingest a data stream of taxi routes in New York City and how to visualize them by using Kibana: *The Essential Guide to Streaming-first Processing with Apache Flink* (*https://www.mapr.com/blog/essential-guide-streaming-first-processing-apache-flink*).

To dig further, data Artisans maintains a free, comprehensive Flink training resource, with all slides, exercises, and solutions as open source. You can find that at *http://dataartisans.github.io/flink-training/*.

More on Time and Windows

A large part of this book has discussed various aspects of time and windows with regard to how Flink works and your choices in using it. Aspects of these topics have also been discussed in a series of blog posts. If you are curious to know more about how Flink windows work, visit *http://flink.apache.org/news/2015/12/04/Introducing-windows.html*, and for more details on session windows, go to *http://data-artisans.com/session-windowing-in-flink/*. If you really want to dig deep into Flink's window and watermark mechanism as well as get an idea of what applications event time is good for, visit *http://data-artisans.com/how-apache-flink-enables-new-streaming-applications-part-1/*.

More on Flink's State and Checkpointing

For Flink's checkpointing and how it compares with older mechanisms to ensure fault-tolerant stream processing, visit *http://data-artisans.com/high-throughput-low-latency-and-exactly-once-stream-processing-with-apache-flink/*.

To learn more about Flink's savepoints, watch this short "Whiteboard Walkthrough" video in which Stephan Ewen describes how to use savepoints to replay streaming data. Savepoints are useful to let you reprocess data, do bug fixes, and do updates. You can watch the video at *https://www.mapr.com/blog/savepoints-apache-flink-stream-processing-whiteboard-walkthrough*.

For additional information about savepoints, head to *http://data-artisans.com/how-apache-flink-enables-new-streaming-applications/*. Also, to view a Whiteboard Walkthrough that presents the benefits and applications of Flink's savepoints, go to *https://www.mapr.com/blog/savepoints-apache-flink-stream-processing-whiteboard-walkthrough*.

To see all these in action in the extension of the Yahoo! benchmark, visit *http://data-artisans.com/extending-the-yahoo-streaming-benchmark/*.

Handling Batch Processing with Flink

To get an idea of how a stream processor can handle batch processing as well, visit *http://data-artisans.com/batch-is-a-special-case-of-streaming.*

There is a lot of information at the Flink blog on the specific mechanisms that Flink uses to optimize batch processing. If you'd like to dig deep into this, we recommend the following:

- *http://flink.apache.org/news/2015/05/11/Juggling-with-Bits-and-Bytes.html*
- *http://flink.apache.org/news/2015/03/13/peeking-into-Apache-Flinks-Engine-Room.html*
- *http://data-artisans.com/computing-recommendations-at-extreme-scale-with-apache-flink/*

Flink Use Cases and User Stories

Companies that are using Flink on a regular basis publish articles on what they achieve with the system and how they are using it. Below is a small selection of links of such user stories:

- *https://techblog.king.com/rbea-scalable-real-time-analytics-king/*
- *https://tech.zalando.de/blog/apache-showdown-flink-vs.-spark/*
- *http://data-artisans.com/flink-at-bouygues-html/*
- *http://data-artisans.com/how-we-selected-apache-flink-at-otto-group/*

The Flink Forward conference series publishes most videos and slides of its talks online, which is a great resource to learn more about what companies are doing with Flink:

- Flink Forward 2015: *http://2015.flink-forward.org/*
- Flink Forward 2016: *http://2016.flink-forward.org/*

Stream-First Architecture

A good place to get more information about stream-based architecture and the message-transport technologies Apache Kafka and MapR Streams is in the book *Streaming Architecture* by Ted Dunning and Ellen Friedman (*http://bit.ly/1Tj5QEW*) (O'Reilly, 2016).

These two short Whiteboard Walkthrough videos explain the advantages of stream-first architecture to support a microservices approach:

- "Key Requirement for Streaming Platforms: A Micro-Services Advantage": *http://bit.ly/2bMkaNk*
- "Streaming Data: How to Move from State to Flow": *https://www.mapr.com/blog/streaming-data-how-move-state-flow-whiteboard-walkthrough-part-2*

Message Transport: Apache Kafka

If you'd like to experiment with Kafka, you can find sample programs in a blog post on the MapR website: "Getting Started with Sample Programs for Apache Kafka 0.9": *https://www.mapr.com/blog/getting-started-sample-programs-apache-kafka-09*

At this time, several chapters of an early release of a book on Kafka, *Kafka: the Definitive Guide* by Neha Narkhede, Gwen Shapira, and Todd Palino are available at *http://oreil.ly/2aEtzFH*.

Message Transport: MapR Streams

To learn more about the message-transport technology that is an integral part of the MapR Converged Data Platform, see the following resources:

- For an overview of MapR Streams' capabilities, including management at the stream level and geo-distributed stream replication, go to *https://www.mapr.com/products/mapr-streams*.
- For sample programs with MapR Streams (which uses the Kafka API), see "Getting Started with MapR Streams": *https://www.mapr.com/blog/getting-started-sample-programs-mapr-streams*.

- For a brief comparison of transport options, see "Apache Kafka and MapR Streams: Terms, Techniques and New Designs": https://www.mapr.com/blog/apache-kafka-and-mapr-streams-terms-techniques-and-new-designs (*https://www.mapr.com/blog/getting-started-sample-programs-mapr-streams*).

Selected O'Reilly Publications by Ted Dunning and Ellen Friedman

- *Streaming Architecture: New Designs Using Apache Kafka and MapR Streams* (O'Reilly, 2016): *http://oreil.ly/1Tj5QEW*
- *Sharing Big Data Safely: Managing Data Security* (O'Reilly, 2015): *http://oreil.ly/1L5XDGv*
- *Real-World Hadoop* (O'Reilly, 2015): *http://oreil.ly/1U4U2fN*
- *Time Series Databases: New Ways to Store and Access Data* (O'Reilly, 2014): *http://oreil.ly/1ulZnOf*
- *Practical Machine Learning: A New Look at Anomaly Detection* (O'Reilly, 2014): *http://oreil.ly/1qNqKm2*
- *Practical Machine Learning: Innovations in Recommendation* (O'Reilly, 2014): *http://oreil.ly/1qt7riC*

About the Authors

Ellen Friedman is a solutions consultant and well-known speaker and author, currently writing mainly about big data topics. She is a committer for the Apache Drill and Apache Mahout projects. With a PhD in Biochemistry, she has years of experience as a research scientist and has written about a variety of technical topics, including molecular biology, nontraditional inheritance, and oceanography. Ellen is also coauthor of a book of magic-themed cartoons, *A Rabbit Under the Hat* (The Edition House). Ellen is on Twitter as @Ellen_Friedman.

Kostas Tzoumas is cofounder and CEO of data Artisans, the company founded by the original creators of Apache Flink. Kostas is a PMC member of Apache Flink and earned a PhD in Computer Science from Aalborg University with postdoctoral experience at TU Berlin. He is author of a number of technical papers and blog articles on stream processing and other data science topics.

Learn from experts.
Find the answers you need.

Sign up for a **10-day free trial** to get **unlimited access** to all of the content on Safari, including Learning Paths, interactive tutorials, and curated playlists that draw from thousands of ebooks and training videos on a wide range of topics, including data, design, DevOps, management, business—and much more.

Start your free trial at:
oreilly.com/safari

(No credit card required.)